Director's and Officer's Complete Letter Book

Second Edition

OTHER BOOKS BY THE AUTHOR:

Developing a Data Dictionary System, Prentice-Hall

Practical Systems and Procedures Manual, Reston

Resource and Management, Prentice-Hall

Director's and Officer's Complete Letter Book

Second Edition

by Prentice-Hall Editorial Staff

J. A. Van Duyn, Editor

Prentice-Hall, Inc.   Englewood Cliffs, New Jersey

Prentice-Hall International, Inc., *London*
Prentice-Hall of Australia, Pty. Ltd., *Sydney*
Prentice-Hall Canada, Inc., *Toronto*
Prentice-Hall of India Private Ltd., *New Delhi*
Prentice-Hall of Japan, Inc., *Tokyo*
Prentice-Hall of Southeast Asia Pte. Ltd., *Singapore*
Whitehall Books, Ltd., Wellington, *New Zealand*

© 1983 by

PRENTICE-HALL, INC.

Englewood Cliffs, N.J.

20   19   18   17   16   15   14   13

Library of Congress Cataloging in Publication Data

Main entry under title:

Director's and officer's complete letter book.

   1.   Commercial correspondence.   I.   Van Duyn, J.A.,
II.   Prentice-Hall, Inc.
HF5726.D57   1982   651.7′5   83-9039
ISBN   0-13-215467-6   AACR2

Printed in the United States of America

THE EDITOR:

J. A. Van Duyn is a management consultant in computer management and information systems as well as a systems analyst for business and industry. Before becoming a consultant, the editor worked for Stanford Research Institute, Croker Bank Data Processing Center, and Computer Sciences Corporation.

The editor is the author of books for the business and industry fields, among them *Developing a Data Dictionary System, Resource and Management,* and *Practical Systems and Procedures Manual,* all published by Prentice-Hall.

An adjunct faculty member at California State University, Sacramento, she teaches part time. Recipient of an M. A. in English/Language Arts from San Francisco State University, the editor is a member of Data Processing Management Association, the California Writers Association, and the American Business Women Association.

WHAT THIS SECOND EDITION WILL DO FOR YOU

This best-selling model letter handbook has now been updated to reflect the dynamic changes that have taken place in the form, language, and style of business letters during the last two decades.

Moreover, scores of letters have been added to this volume that deal with subjects relating to new technology such as apologizing for computer errors, contracting for hardware and software, and/or computer services; topics that were unheard of when the first edition was published. Each letter is a model of clarity and informality, devoid of excess verbiage and free of legal pitfalls.

This second, expanded edition continues to provide the executive with the latest state-of-the-art in practical, simple-to-use, field-tested letters that deal effectively with every possible situation in today's business environment. Whether your secretary is using a word processing computer or a typewriter, these letters save time, money and manpower.

Because this book covers a large array of timely topics such as how to respond to the media and how to show appreciation for hospitality, just to mention a couple of subjects, it will save you hours of labor searching for the correct phrase, the exact word needed to communicate your thoughts when writing difficult letters. It offers you 133 ready-to-use model letters and 988 alternate phrases and sentences that you can adapt, with hardly any effort, to your own specific situation and needs.

This book will help you to ensure that clichés—which at most can destroy the effect of an otherwise impressive letter; at minimum annoy the reader—do not slip into your written communications. In summation, this is not a book on letter-writing techniques. Rather, it's a collection of well-written, result-producing letters from successful executives that can be easily adapted to your own unique requirements.

The following pinpoints the value of each chapter's carefully selected, field-tested letters and alternate phrases and sentences. They are arranged within a particular category to best serve you, the busy executive. Each group of letters is followed by General Rules, which enable you to check key points in your own letters. These rules can be put in a pamphlet or policy guide as an aid for your secretary or assistant.

• Scores of proven, individual letters for special situations. These include letters to public officials, legislators, lecturers, program chairpersons, and organizations, as well as letters accepting or declining speaking invitations and appointive positions. Also, letters requesting permission to use published material, and more. (See Chapter 1.)

• Sample annual report letters by the president, letters welcoming new stockholders, letters describing the latest stockholders' meeting, and other key correspondence directed to shareholders. (See Chapter 2.)

• Difficult-to-write letters of sympathy, apology, and congratulations, as well as letters asking for charitable contributions, refusal to lend name to fund-raising drive, voicing opinion to a particular media, and hospitality letters. (See Chapter 3.)

• Effective letters for welcoming new customer, thanking customer for business suggestion, and complimenting a good account, as well as letters apologizing for action of employee, computer error, or service department. (See Chapter 4.)

• Key letters for requesting information from vendor, cover letters for Request for Proposal (RFP) or Request for Quotation (RFQ), letters accepting or rejecting submitted proposals, letters renewing or canceling contracts or orders, and more. (See Chapter 5.)

• Field-tested letters to bankers, financial institutions, government agencies, overseas contracts. (See Chapter 6.)

• Letters for answering information request about the company products, requesting appointment with a potential customer/client, follow-up and follow-through sales letters, introducing new salesperson, and other critical marketing and sales correspondence. (See Chapter 7.)

• Letters to grant credit terms, turn down credit applicant, a broad range of collection letters, letters of apology for collection letter sent in error, and unearned discount letters. (See Chapter 8.)

• Letters for accepting offers to get involved in community activities, refusing offers to get involved in community activities on a personal or company basis, and contributing to charity. (See Chapter 9.)

• Sample letters to the local and national press, radio, and TV to correct misinformation about the company, as well as letters to congratulate, criticize, make a point, or take a position on something that appeared in print or was broadcast on TV or radio about the company or the particular field in which it operates. (See Chapter 10.)

• Tested letters to welcome new employees, turn down a job applicant, invite employee suggestions, offer sympathy when employee is ill or injured, inform employees of imminent merger and explain its effect on employees. (See Chapter 11.)

• Helpful guidance in simple, easy-to-follow steps—with ample examples —so that your letters will have an elegant, uncluttered look that enhances the effectiveness of your text. (See Chapter 12.)

• Appendix A—Complete Master Letter Checklist helps you to avoid the usual pitfalls that can complicate business letter writing. For ease of use as a reference checklist, it is organized in alphabetical order. It includes the proper Address Form, Complimentary Close, Salutation, Style, and Tone, to mention some of the items discussed.

• Appendix B—Proper Address Forms provides time-saving, useful charts in displaying the correct address forms, salutation, and complimentary close to be used in letters to persons with official titles.

A conscious effort has been made in this second edition to make the contents of this book even more comprehensive, even more convenient for the reader. Consequently, the sample letters appear on the right pages, and the general rules and alternate phrases appear on the left pages for ready use in the firing line of business.

Need a letter? Turn to the table of contents and select the letter you want within the particular category. Take the letter as is, adapt it to fit your needs, or choose the alternate paragraphs that best serve your purpose. All in all, you will find this second edition of *Director's and Officer's Complete Letter Book* an invaluable reference guide and an excellent time-saving tool.

J. A. Van Duyn

Contents

4. TACTFUL LETTERS FOR PROMOTING EFFECTIVE CUSTOMER RELATIONS 95

5. TASTEFUL LETTERS FOR CONTRACTING AND DEALING WITH PRODUCTS AND/OR SERVICES 125

6. PRODUCTIVE LETTERS THAT DEAL WITH FINANCIAL MATTERS 143

1

Special Letters for Challenging Situations

While you may find that many letters in this book can be used for special situations, there are some that are worthy of separate treatment because of their distinctive nature. These include letters to public officials, legislators, speakers or lecturers, program chairpersons, organizations and associations; letters accepting or declining speaking invitations; accepting or declining elective or appointive positions, as well as letters requesting permission to use published material.

Please note that formal, stilted letters are a thing of the past. Even when dealing with government officials, you don't bore them with ceremonious language; you use the same crisp, direct language and style you use in any other business letter.

The letters in this chapter and throughout the book respond to the specific circumstances, allowing for minor adjustments to cover different situations. Change a few key words and you have the right letter for the right situation.

• LETTER TO PUBLIC OFFICIAL

Your public officials can do much more for you if they know you and are aware of your concerns. They will appreciate your writing a letter to them whenever an important event or issue comes up. Letters dealing with other matters are also included.

General Rules

Be specific and concise in stating your message, and, if possible, compliment the person to whom you are writing.

Make sure that you are using the correct form of address. (See Appendix B.)

Alternate Phrases

(a) Thank you for your prompt reply to our letter of May 20. The wine industry is very pleased that you are going to assist us in some of our foreign trade problems. We also appreciate your submitting appropriate recommendations to the other government agencies involved in this matter.

As president of the Better City Government Club, it is my pleasure to tell you that the members voted unanimously to make you honorary chairman of our club. This is our way of showing you how pleased our community is with the way you are fulfilling your office.

Without a doubt, the life of a public official is rather difficult at times. I also know that there is always more than one approach to solving a problem. However, in a case where the resulting solution is obviously wrong, the whole problem should be reconsidered.

(b) We are glad to respond to your request to give you, in writing, the factors which make a commodity agreement acceptable to other countries, and our suggestions as to the modification of the Zurich agreement. The information will be sent to you shortly.

It is not often that a community like ours gets a public official who really cares about citizens and tries to improve the community. We are also aware that certain sectors in our community do not give you the cooperation you need. Our club is starting a campaign to alleviate that problem.

We feel very strongly that the conclusion your department arrived at, namely, to motorize the police, is endangering our community. Since the foot patrol persons have left, hoodlums have moved in and crime has climbed at a frightening rate.

(c) Because of the assurances in your letter, our industry is more confident now of the possibility of countering excessive amounts of foreign imports, and of developing agreements for exports of our products to various countries.

Keep up the excellent work. We, the concerned citizens, appreciate it.

If you will examine the situation you have only one course of action: reinstate the foot patrol.

DESK-TOP COMPUTERS, INC.

FRONTAGE ROAD

STARK VIEW, TEXAS

XXXXXXXXXXXXXX
XXXXXXXXXXXXXX
XXXXXXXXXXXXXX

Dear Jordan:

Please accept my congratulations on your appointment by our Mayor to be the Chief of Police. Your capabilities and expertise as an administrator and a crime-fighter will be a great value in carrying out the heavy responsibility of making our city safe once again.

I believe that I speak not only for myself but for the whole business community when I say that you can be sure of our full cooperation and support.

Please don't hesitate to call on us if we can be of any assistance in the important work that lies ahead of you.

Cordially,

DESK-TOP COMPUTERS, Inc.
Charles R. Marsh
President

Letter to Public Official

• LETTER TO LEGISLATOR

If you are interested in a bill, then a letter to your congress person telling him or her how you feel, and why, is in order. A lawmaker wants to know what his/her constituents are thinking, and will be especially appreciative if the letter contains facts and figures.

General Rules

State the subject of your letter and your position in the opening paragraph. If you have a recommendation to make, be as brief and specific as possible.

Alternate Phrases

(a) It is my understanding that the Wilderness Bill, which I firmly believe is vital to our country's preservation of natural resources, is still in the Public Lands Subcommittee.

Thank you for your letter of September 21, relative to the Gore amendments to H.R. 10.

Thank you for your prompt reply of July 22. I certainly appreciate the problem you have of convincing your colleagues of the need for more funds to fight the air pollution menace in our state.

(b) Acting upon this assumption, I'm sending you a copy of the letter which I sent some time ago to one of your colleagues. If you will review the facts in my letter, I am sure you will arrive at the proper solution.

We are pleased to learn from the media that these amendments were rejected in the committee. Your opposition was undoubtedly an important contributing factor in the committee's final decision.

(c) I appreciate that you share my concern about this serious situation, and you can count on my continued support.

Your response to our telegram is sincerely appreciated.

If there is any way that I can be of any assistance to you in this fight please call upon me.

PEOPLE FOR ANIMAL RIGHTS, INC.

278 DARTMOUTH AVE.

SAN CARLOS, CALIFORNIA

Senator _____
United States Senate
Washington, D.C. 20510

Dear Senator:

Because I read in the paper that you have become a cosponsor of S.2619, the Fur Seal Protection Act, I'm writing to relay to you our organization's concern for the Pribilof seals, and our support for bill S.2619.

Through the media, we have been trying to educate the public about the background of this annual wholesale destruction of seals. Besides you and certain concerned groups, very few people seem to know that under the terms of a 1957 agreement (a revision of a 1911 convention) between United States, Japan, Russia, and Canada, Japan and Canada get 15% of the seal skins taken commercially by the U.S., and that U.S.S.R. gets control of all the breeding areas off the north Asian coast. As a result of this international agreement, 30,000 seals are clubbed to death EACH YEAR by the Aleut Indians on Pribilof Islands, U.S.A.

Notwithstanding the fact that the seal population has plunged from 5 million to 1.8 million, it is our understanding that the Department of State, responsible for the renegotiation of this convention, fully intends for the U.S. to continue participation in this needless slaughter of wildlife. They claim that this is done to "maintain the Pribilof seal population at approximately 2 million."

We who believe that animals have a right to live also do not accept this argument and intend to fight it.

We appreciate your being a cosponsor of S.2619, and you can be assured of our full support.

Sincerely,

PEOPLE FOR ANIMAL RIGHTS, Inc.
Don F. McAlpin
President

Letter to Legislator

• LETTER TO A PROGRAM CHAIRPERSON

If you have enjoyed a convention, a conference, or a seminar, you should write and compliment the program chairperson. As you know, organizing and managing such an event entails a lot of effort, and the person who does it well deserves some praise.

General Rules

The tone of this letter should be sincere and appreciative.
Name something specific that especially pleased you.

Alternate Phrases

(a) The convention held last week in St. Louis was just about the best I have ever attended. While I realize that the efforts of many people are involved in such an affair, the program chairperson can make a good convention great. And you did just that.

Well, Richard, you did it again. You came through with another excellent seminar. And I, along with everyone of the attendees I met, applaud you for it.

Our recent conference in San Francisco was truly enjoyable. You did a fine job as program chairman. Congratulations for making this event a memorable occasion.

(b) Many conventioneers and their wives spoke to me and called me later about the fine hotel accommodations and sightseeing tours you arranged for them. They asked me to thank you for an especially pleasant visit to our city.

The intelligent and creative arrangements you have made for meetings, guest lecturers, and entertainment is the talk of our profession. We knew you could do it, but we didn't know you would do it so well.

(c) We hope you will accept to do the same fine job for our next convention.

I expect to be in your city some time next month and look forward to congratulating you in person.

Again, congratulations on a great job. We hope you will do it again next year.

NEW ENGLAND INVESTMENT COMPANY

910 QUEENS AVENUE

ALBANY, N.Y.

XXXXXXXXXXXXXX
XXXXXXXXXXXXXX
XXXXXXXXXXXXXX

Dear Glenn:

Last week's DELPHI convention in Chicago was most enjoyable. Through your efforts as program chairman, we not only had interesting and knowledgeable speakers, but all events went smoothly and according to schedule.

My wife wants you to know how much she, too, enjoyed the convention. She thought that the side trips and entertainment you arranged for the ladies were outstanding.

It was good to see you. I hope we can get together for lunch on my next trip to New York City.

Cordially,

Letter to a Program Chairperson

• INVITATION TO A SPEAKER

Most people are pleased to be invited to speak at a business, academic, or social function. A gracious letter giving the necessary details is often all you need to persuade the recipient to accept your invitation.

General Rules

Tell the prospective speaker the subject matter of the speech or the area in which you would like him or her to speak.

Compliment the speaker on his or her qualifications to talk on the subject.

State the time, place, and length of speech, and if the club, association, or college can pay an honorarium.

Impress upon the speaker how welcome he or she will be.

Alternate Phrases

(a) Your article in this month's *Fortune* magazine was fascinating.

So many people told me about the outstanding talk you gave before the Celts a couple of days ago, that I'd be delighted if you could give the same at our annual meeting.

The program committee is hard at work on arrangements for the annual meeting of the Professional Women in Data Processing. We are inviting the participation of women who are outstanding computer professionals in various industries.

(b) A talk based on your published article would make a most entertaining and informative presentation on the growing computer games market abroad. I am, therefore, inviting you to speak informally to the American Computer Association's March 3 lunch meeting.

This meeting will be held at the Biltmore Hotel on November 18, at 8:00 p.m. The subject of solar energy is one of much interest to such groups as ours, and I know you would make a real hit with it.

It is for this reason I am writing to you. Members of the committee have decided unanimously that you are the ideal professional woman to address the meeting on the subject of new vistas for women.

(c) I hope your schedule will permit your acceptance, for I know that our members would be delighted to hear and learn about this opportunity abroad for business people.

If you can be with us on this date, I shall announce the good news at next week's meeting. I can assure you that we will have a peak attendance to hear you.

In view of your experience and accomplishments in this field, the audience would greatly appreciate the privilege to hear you discuss this important subject. We plan the talk for 8:00 p.m. at The Plaza on May 2.

R&W REALTY COMPANY

445 CARRIAGE HILL ROAD

TARRYVILLE, VERMONT

XXXXXXXXXXXXXX
XXXXXXXXXXXXXX
XXXXXXXXXXXXXX

Dear Mr. Schwartz:

The subject of "Effective Written Communications" is of interest to every business and professional person. You, of course, know this better than either me or my colleagues, since you have written a book and several articles for leading business magazines on the subject.

As Program Chairman of the local Professional Realtors Association, I would like to invite you to be our speaker at our next meeting on November 17. It would be a pleasure to have a person of your caliber and expertise give us a presentation on this timely subject. The honorarium we can offer is moderate, but it will cover your traveling expenses.

Our dinner meetings are held in the Fireside Room of Hotel Cleveland. Happy hour starts at 6:30 p.m., dinner at 7:30 p.m., and the presentation usually begins around 8:15 or 8:30 p.m. The talk generally ranges from 30 to 45 minutes, followed by a questions and answers period.

If you can find it possible to accept my invitation for November 17, you will receive a most enthusiastic welcome from the members of our association.

Sincerely,

Invitation to a Speaker

(d) (This paragraph may be omitted.)

I sincerely hope that you will be able to accept our invitation. If you can, please let me know what your terms are, and whether you will need any special equipment.

• ACCEPTING AN INVITATION TO SPEAK

The letter accepting an invitation should be courteous and appreciative. If the invitation has not mentioned the topic or the specific time, the acceptance must deal with these points.

General Rules

Show that you are glad to be invited.
Specify or confirm the time and subject of your presentation.

Alternate Phrases

(a) I shall be happy to speak to the Retail Marketing Association at their dinner meeting on October 9 in the Redwood Room of Holiday Inn. Thank you for asking me.

It will be a pleasure to speak before the Lions on January 5. I'm happy to be able to accept your invitation.

Your inviting me to speak before the Elks on March 7 is a compliment. I accept with pleasure.

(b) The subject you suggest is quite satisfactory, and I shall do my best to give your members an interesting half an hour.

Recently, before a group of Rotarians, I spoke on "Personal Computers, the Next Major Home Appliance." Would this topic be appropriate for your meeting?

Because of recent developments, I have updated the content of my speech. I hope this material will be of interest and help to the members of your group.

(c) (This paragraph may be omitted.)

I shall be glad to meet you in the Hilton Hotel at 7:30 p.m. I look forward to visiting your club.

You deserve a lot of credit for the fine work you are doing in the field of energy conservation. I hope my presentation will contribute toward your efforts.

It will be a pleasure to visit with the members of your association, many of whom I know.

WINE INSTITUTE

717 MARKET STREET

SAN FRANCISCO, CALIFORNIA

XXXXXXXXXXXXXX
XXXXXXXXXXXXXX
XXXXXXXXXXXXXX

Dear Mr. Syngleton:

Thank you for asking me to give another talk at your Napa Host Breakfast, Friday, February 5, on the "Success of California Wine in Europe."

Because of a scheduled late meeting I won't be able to attend the reception Thursday evening. However, I will be driving up early Friday morning to be on time for the breakfast and my speech.

I am looking forward to seeing you and your colleagues again.

Cordially,

WINE INSTITUTE
Frank Bell
President

Accepting an Invitation to Speak

• DECLINING AN APPOINTIVE OR ELECTIVE POSITION

The letter declining an appointive or elective position should be tactful and sincere.

General Rules

Make clear the reason why you cannot accept the position offered.
If appropriate, ask to be considered for other positions in the future.

Alternate Phrases

(a) It was good of you to offer me the Treasurer position in your club.

Your offering me the position of Program Coordinator in your nonprofit organization is a very nice gesture.

Thank you for asking me to serve on your board of advisors for Better Community Colleges.

(b) Regretfully, I have to decline the offer because my schedule is so full already that I hardly have time for my family.

I am truly sorry, but I cannot accept your offer. My business travels take me out of town so often that I could never be sure of being able to attend your organization's meetings, nor of fulfilling the responsibilities of a program coordinator.

While I realize the importance of serving on your board, I'm afraid that I have to decline the offer. My family made me promise that on account of recent health problems I wouldn't take on any more responsibilities.

(c) Thanks again. I appreciate your thinking of me.

Best wishes to you.

I know you will understand my family's concern.

MONROE BANK

MONROE PLAZA

MOUNTAIN GROVE, N.Y.

XXXXXXXXXXXXXX
XXXXXXXXXXXXX
XXXXXXXXXXXXX

Gentlemen:

Thank you for offering me the chairman's position in the Professional Bankers Association, New York Branch.

While I am honored that a nationally known and respected association like the PBA thought of me, regretfully, I have to decline the offer.

My position as vice president here at the bank, and my responsibilities as head of the local school board and participation in other civic organizations take 100% of my time.

Thank you again for thinking of me. I appreciate it.

Sincerely,

Declining an Appointive or Elective Position

• COMPLIMENTING A LECTURER OR SPEAKER

Every speaker likes to know that his or her efforts were well received. A brief note complimenting the speaker, and thanking him or her for an interesting presentation will be appreciated by the addressed person.

General Rules

State the name of the organization if the letterhead does not indicate it, or the title of the speech the addressee gave.

Express the appreciation of the entire group or organization.

Alternate Phrases

(a)   The National League for Safe Highways wishes to express appreciation to you for the interesting and constructive talk you gave on Monday evening.

Thank you ever so much for a stimulating speech. The League of Women Voters will long remember the enthusiasm you generated by your original approach to a complicated subject.

The ABC Club members want to thank you again for the informative talk you gave last week. It has been a long time since we had a speaker with your expertise on the "Law and Order" issue.

(b)   Because of your in-depth knowledge and ability to discuss the various aspects of this problem, we will long remember this evening.

While it is just a few days since your talk, many of our members have already taken steps to put some of your ideas into action. We look forward of having you speak again in the near future.

It was the best event of the series. We hope you will honor us again with a presentation next year.

(c)   (This paragraph may be omitted.)

Once again, thank you for speaking at our monthly meeting and for making that evening so enjoyable.

Our group wants to thank you for giving us a most entertaining talk. We all hope that you will return to our city soon, so that once again we can have the pleasure of having you at one of our meetings.

BPI COMMUNICATIONS, INC.

475 TERRACE AVENUE

MINNEAPOLIS, MINNESOTA

XXXXXXXXXXXXXXX
XXXXXXXXXXXXXX
XXXXXXXXXXXXXX

Dear Dr. Bradley:

Your lecture on the "Next Wave of the Future" at our symposium last week was informative and interesting. In fact, your imaginative presentation was the highlight of the symposium.

The audience, including myself, enjoyed very much the "sneak preview" you provided us about the future global communications. The standing ovation given to you at the end of your speech reflected the consensus.

All of us at the symposium thank you for an outstanding presentation. We hope that you will be able to come again next year.

Cordially,

Complimenting a Lecturer or Speaker

• DECLINING AN INVITATION TO SPEAK

The letter declining an invitation to speak should be appreciative and straightforward but tactful.

General Rules

Tell exactly what prevents you from accepting the invitation.
If you wish to be considered for a future appearance, state it so.

Alternate Phrases

(a) I appreciate your gracious invitation, and if I were to accept any invitation to make a speech, I would certainly accept yours.

I am truly sorry that I can't accept your invitation, as I'm scheduled to be the main speaker at the American Business Management symposium on October 5.

Thank you for asking me to the semi-annual meeting of the Masons as the guest of honor. Speaking to your group would be a great pleasure, and I would like nothing better than to accept your invitation.

(b) Several months ago, however, for health reasons I made up my mind to cut down on extracurricular activities, including speech making.

I can assure you that were the speaking engagement not made three months ago, it would have been a pleasure to accept your invitation.

Unfortunately, however, on June 9 my company has scheduled a board of directors' meeting which, I know from past experience, will last all day.

(c) I am now chairman of the board, and the younger men and women in the company are the ones who accept invitations to speak to various organizations.

I certainly regret that I'm booked on that date and that I will miss meeting you and your group. Perhaps I can make it to your next conference.

I hope you give me a rain check on this invitation because I would enjoy visiting with you and your group.

INVESTMENT INSURANCE COMPANY

950 GOLDEN OAK AVENUE

HOLLAND, MICHIGAN

XXXXXXXXXXXXXXX
XXXXXXXXXXXXXX
XXXXXXXXXXXXX

Dear Mr. Norden:

It was good of you to invite me to give the commencement address at Middlebury High School. Visiting a school like yours that enjoys a national reputation for progressive methods, effective programs, and outstanding graduates would be a pleasure.

Unfortunately, however, my schedule doesn't allow me to accept your kind invitation. Fact of the matter is that I will be out of town attending an international conference the whole week of May 28.

I appreciate your thinking of me, and I hope you will keep me in mind for future occasions.

Sincerely,

Declining an Invitation to Speak

• PRAISING STAFF (HOTEL OR OUTSIDE COMPANY)

Not too many people write this type of letter, yet a brief note of compliment, or a few words of appreciation is well worth the effort because it creates lasting goodwill.

General Rules

Be specific about what motivated you to write the letter.
Be gracious but don't gush when complimenting the staff.

Alternate Phrases

(a) Thanks to your efficient staff, the convention of the Retail Market Association held last week in your hotel was a success.

The Christmas party we had a few days ago in the El Capitan Room of your hotel was the best ever.

Our exhibit of the Contemporary American Artists in the Rembrandt room of your restaurant turned out to be more profitable than we hoped for.

(b) Specifically, it was the personal attention that you and your courteous, well-trained staff gave to the details that made everything run smoothly. Your staff's efforts to please were gratifying and much appreciated by our entire membership.

We know that this didn't happen just by accident. Consequently, we would like to congratulate you and your staff for making this a memorable party. Each one of your staff deserves an accolade for his or her courtesy, efficiency, and pleasant disposition.

A large part of credit goes to you and your staff for the fine cooperation you have all displayed.

(c) Because our convention was so successful, we would like to reserve the same dates for our 35th annual convention next year. Please send me a confirmation as soon as possible.

Please convey my compliments to your staff. We are looking forward to our next affair at your hotel.

Since I cannot possibly compliment each one of your staff personally, I would appreciate your showing them this letter. Thank you.

WINE INSTITUTE

717 MARKET STREET

SAN FRANCISCO, CALIFORNIA

XXXXXXXXXXXXXX
XXXXXXXXXXXXXX
XXXXXXXXXXXXXX

Dear Mr. Simon:

For the past year we have been holding our monthly meeting in the Banquet Room of your hotel. As we are going into our second year at this location, it seems like the proper time to compliment you and your staff for the excellent food and service we have had at each and every one of our meetings.

Please extend to all your employees who work in the Banquet Room, and to your chef and his staff in the kitchen, our sincere thanks and appreciation.

Sincerely,

Praising Staff (Hotel or Outside Company)

• REQUESTING PERMISSION TO USE PUBLISHED MATERIAL

If a manuscript you are preparing is going to contain direct quotations, paraphrases, condensations, synopses, charts, tables, or illustrations from copyrighted publications, or unpublished letters, speeches, photographs, or dissertations, you will need permission from the appropriate person.

General Rules

Send the letter in duplicate, so that the addressee can keep one copy and return the other.

Be specific about the material you wish to use, the publication in which it appears, and the page number, if appropriate.

Tell exactly how you are going to use the material.

MARVIE REPORTS CORPORATION

200 SPENCER AVENUE

CHICAGO, ILLINOIS

XXXXXXXXXXXXXX
XXXXXXXXXXXXXX
XXXXXXXXXXXXXX

Gentlemen:

We are preparing a text on real estate investment opportunities to be published next January. Because an article in the September issue of your magazine, **Horizons**, is relevant to our topic, we would like to reproduce it in our forthcoming book.

The title of the article is "Mountain Retreats," and it is by Don Smythe. The author, as well as your publication, will get full credit in the chapter using the above article.

We would greatly appreciate your permission to use this material. For your convenience, a release form in two copies is attached. Please sign and mail the original in our self-addressed stamped envelope, and keep the copy for your files.

Thank you for your cooperation.

Sincerely,

Requesting Permission to Use Published Material

Gentlemen:

    I am writing a textbook on _____ to be published by _____. May I please have your permission to include the following material from

_____

_____

        By _____

for use in my book and in future revisions and editions?

    Unless you indicate otherwise, I propose to use the following credit line:

    Through the courtesy of _____.

    Your consent to this request will be deeply appreciated.

    For your convenience a release form is given below, and a copy of this letter is enclosed for your files.

                                     Sincerely,

                                 _____

. . . .

    I (we) grant permission for the use of the material requested above.

                              _____

                      By _____

Date _____

Alternate Letter

Informative Letters
to Stockholders

2

Letters written to stockholders of public corporations primarily concern themselves with corporate revenue gain or loss. Whether they introduce the annual or quarterly report, deal with corporate structural or financial changes, or notify the shareholders of annual or special meetings, these letters inform as well as promote good relations.

This chapter includes samples of most types of letters you will need when writing to your shareholders. All you need to do is fill in the pertinent data.

• ANNUAL REPORT LETTER

The Prime Computer letter on the opposite page is an excellent example of what an effective annual report letter can be.

General Rules

Make it personalized. Include a photograph of yourself (if you are the chairperson) and/or of the president and executive officer (if you are the latter). Make sure that the signature(s) are prominently displayed at the end of the report.

Make it informal. Simple language and direct approach will get more shareholders to read the letter and feel involved with the progress of their company than by using pompous language and formal style. If you have reason to be pleased with your company's management, employees, and progress, say so.

Conversely, don't try to paint an artificially rosy picture. If there is any bad news pertaining to the company's revenue, say it boldly at the very beginning of your letter. This creates the favorable impression that management is not trying to hide something, and that the shareholders are getting an accurate account of how their company is doing.

Make sure that the data you impart are not just a rehash of figures from charts on later pages. Your shareholders will read your letter if the information you give cannot be found anywhere else in the annual or quarterly report.

Alternate Phrases

(a) The results of fiscal year 19—— were encouraging. Your Company proved its soundness and resilience by recovering quickly from the difficulties experienced in the last two quarters of the previous year.

   During the 19—— fiscal year ABC Incorporated recorded a net loss of $1.5 million on revenues of $130.2 million. This loss, the first in our six years of operating history, compares to net income of $2.6 million on revenues of $128.3 in the previous fiscal year.

(b) We're especially pleased with management's successful efforts to lower operating and administrative expenses through the newly implemented measurement and control system.

   In the face of these losses, your management decided to embark on a rigorous "tighten operations" program. This meant cutting both operating and administrative expenses down to the absolute minimum. This was a painful but necessary action that should bring positive results this fiscal year.

(c) We are proud of what our management and employees have accomplished this fiscal year. Moreover, the results prove once again not only that our Company is

PRIME COMPUTER, INC.

40 WALNUT STREET

WELLESLEY HILLS, MASSACHUSETTS 02181

XXXXXXXXXXXXXX
XXXXXXXXXXXXXX
XXXXXXXXXXXXXX

To our Shareholders:

Prime Computer had a very good year in 19 — —. Sales grew more than 60% and net income doubled. Your management and Board of Directors continuously measure the performance of Prime against that of our competitors and U.S. business in general. We are pleased to report that every analysis of competitive performance we've seen in recent years evidences the soundness and vitality of your company.

Prime's performance relative to its industry and principal competitors is the best evidence available of the quality of our management. We, your Board, believe that Prime has a truly superior management group with excellent performance in each area of its operations. In the early years of Prime, we recruited executives to head each functional area who had managed groups much larger in size than the groups they initially managed at Prime.

This approach allowed Prime to grow at high annual rates without putting undue pressure on our management. Our strategy worked, with the result that we've had less turnover of senior management than most other high growth companies in our industry. We've shown consistently superior performance in our industry as measured by any objective standards. Prime's performance obviously reflects the competence not only of the senior officers but also that of all our managers and employees. We are very proud of the accomplishments of our entire organization and know that you, our shareholders, share this pride.

A major responsibility of your Board is to maintain an identity of interests among the management and employees of Prime and its shareholders. We believe that we've done this to good effect through our stock purchase, profit sharing and stock option plans.

Through the courtesy of Prime Computer, Inc., Prime Park, Natick, MA 01760

Annual Report Letter

built on a solid basis, but that it is flexible and can get back on the road to success after a short detour.

Your board truly believes that the actions taken this year, along with the strengthening of senior and middle management, will make ABC Corporation once again the profitable enterprise for its management and shareholders that it has been for the past six years.

In our stock purchase plan, we allow each employee to set aside up to 10% of his/her salary to purchase stock at 85% of the lesser of its price at the beginning or end of the year. We are very pleased that 75.1% of our employees participated in this plan this year. Under our Management Incentive Plan, our six highest salaried executives received more than 60% of their cash compensation from profit sharing this year. In total, more than 175 employees participated in profit sharing. We also issued a considerable number of stock options to key employees during this year. These options were issued to a total of 260 employees, and reflected a considered judgment by your Board to recognize the outstanding performance of the recipients while providing them with a long-term incentive to maintain their relationship with your Company.

As you know, your Board of Directors has a strong majority of independent, non-management directors. We spend considerable time in the design and implementation of our various profit sharing and incentive plans, always with the end purpose in mind of enhancing the value of your investment. We believe that we've achieved this end, and that our programs for providing equitable incentive to officers and employees have contributed significantly to your Company's success.

Your Board is pleased with the accomplishments of 19— —, and is confident that Prime's officers and employees will attain the ambitious goals for continued growth in sales and earnings we have established.

For the Board of Directors,

David J. Dunn
Chairman

Annual Report Letter (continued)

• WELCOME LETTER TO NEW SHAREHOLDER

A letter welcoming a new shareholder can create goodwill, enhance the company's public image, and be an effective sales letter. Remember that your new shareholders may be actual or potential customers.

General Rules

Make it an individual letter, one that reflects your personality and sincerity.

Make the shareholder feel part of the company. Using the words "you" and "our" can help do this.

If appropriate, tell him or her about your products.

Alternate Phrases

(a) It is a pleasure to welcome you as a stockholder in our Company.

On behalf of our directors and executive officers, I am pleased to welcome you as a shareholder of National Chemicals, Inc.

(b) To keep you informed about the Company's operations and financial status, we are sending you, under separate cover, a copy of our latest annual report.

You will receive our regular quarterly and annual reports, and any special notices that will be issued. Through these communications we intend to keep you informed about our Company.

(c) I trust that you will find your new association with our Company satisfactory in every way.

If you would like additional information on our Company's specific products or on any of our various divisions and subsidiaries, please let us know.

(d) We are always interested in any comments you may have pertaining to our operations.

BROWN, KING & WOOD, INC.

NASHVILLE, TENNESSEE

XXXXXXXXXXXXXX
XXXXXXXXXXXXXX
XXXXXXXXXXXXXX

Dear Ms _____:

I want to welcome you as a shareholder of Brown, King & Wood, Inc. You can be sure that we will do our best to fulfill our obligation to you as an investor in our Company.

Since a service organization is only as good as its people, we firmly believe that our efficient, quality management will continue to show increasing sales and profit in our widespread set of operations. Because of these factors, we are looking forward to a long and pleasant association between you and our Company.

Enclosed please find our latest annual report and quarterly financial report. We would be pleased to get any comments, suggestions, or questions from you.

Very truly yours,

Welcome Letter to New Shareholder

• SPECIAL LETTER TO FORMER SHAREHOLDER

When a large block of your company stocks is sold, it is usually nothing more than a normal stock transaction and does not indicate any dissatisfaction with your company. Nevertheless, writing a goodwill letter to a former shareholder is worth the effort because if the holder of the stocks happens to be a customer, it can help keep him or her as a customer. Moreover, whether the former shareholder is a customer or not, it may persuade him or her to invest again in your company stock.

General Rules

Express your appreciation for the addressee's having been a shareholder in your company. Offer to continue sending the company's annual and quarterly reports. Invite comments and/or suggestions regarding your company's policies and operations.

Alternate Phrases

(a) Our records indicate that you are no longer a shareholder in our Company. We are sorry about that, especially since your participation in ABC was greatly appreciated. We sincerely hope to have the pleasure of welcoming you back as one of our shareholders in the near future.

Your participation in our Company as a shareholder was appreciated, and we regret that you found it necessary to dispose of your ABC stocks.

(b) If the decision to dispose of your ABC stocks was on account of the recent changes in our Company's policies, I hope you will write me about it. In the meantime, if you would like to continue to receive ABC's financial reports, please let me know.

Because we believe that former shareholders remain interested in the increasing revenues and growth of our Company, we are pleased to continue sending you our reports.

(c) Occasionally, shareholders transfer their holdings into the name of a broker who is managing their account under some form of instructions. If this is the case, please disregard the above, and let me thank you for your continued expression of confidence in our Company.

It will be a pleasure to welcome you back whenever you decide to once again become a shareholder in ABC.

NATIONAL EASTERN OIL CORPORATION

AVENUE OF THE AMERICAS

NEW YORK, N.Y.

XXXXXXXXXXXXXX
XXXXXXXXXXXXXX
XXXXXXXXXXXXXX

Dear Mr. _____:

It has recently come to my attention that your name no longer appears on our books as a shareholder. While I appreciate that sometimes certain events force the shareholder to sell even long-held stocks, it is still a transaction we regret to see.

However, if your decision to dispose of your NEO stocks was related to any aspect of NEO's policies or operations, I would appreciate your letting me know. We value your friendship and hope to retain it even though you are no longer one of our shareholders.

If you would like to receive our future annual and quarterly reports, please let me know. I will be glad to arrange to have your name remain on our mailing list.

Very truly yours,

Keith Donaldson
President and Chief Executive Officer

Special Letter to Former Shareholder

• LETTER DEALING WITH FINANCIAL OR CAPITAL STRUCTURE CHANGES

Whether the letter dealing with financial or capital structure changes is about the sale and liquidation of the company, about a stock split, about the acquisition of the assets of another company, or about the election of new Directors, it is an extremely important communication, and consequently it must be written with great care.

General Rules

Make the letter the quintessence of clearness and conciseness.
Include all pertinent data that concern your shareholders.

Alternate Phrases

(a) At a meeting held on April 18, 19——, the Board of Directors of your Company, subject to the approval of shareholders, authorized a three-for-one stock split.

At a meeting to be held on November 4, 19——, as voted on by officers and shareholders, new Directors will be elected.

(b) To make this possible, at the annual meeting to be held June 5, 19——, the shareholders will be presented with the following resolutions for their approval: The distribution to shareholders, on the record date to be determined later, of two (2) new shares for each share then held, and the transfer to capital from earned surplus of a sum equal to the aggregate par value of the shares so distributed.

In addition to the election of Directors, there will be transaction of other business to be voted on and acted upon.

(c) The proposed stock distribution will not change any shareholder's proportionate interest in the corporation but will triple the number of shares held by him or her.

If you cannot be present at the meeting, please sign and mail the enclosed proxy.

SANDERS CONSTRUCTION COMPANY

JACKSONVILLE, FLORIDA

To the Shareholders:

After many months of discussions your Company has entered into an agreement to sell substantially all of the Company's assets to Plymouth Construction Ltd., of England for $35 million cash.

While we, the undersigned, James I. Dermott, Chairman of the Board, and Ron S. Diamond, President, have agreed to vote our collective shares of more than 40 percent of the Company's stock in favor of the sale and liquidation, the sale agreement is subject to the approval of our shareholders.

Consequently, we are calling a special meeting of the shareholders to be held on January 7, 19— — at 10 a.m. at the Company's office. At that time all the conditions of the above sale will be discussed (including the fact that Plymouth Construction Ltd., will assume certain liabilities, such as taxes) and voted on.

If you cannot be present at the meeting, please date, sign and return the proxy in the enclosed self-addressed stamped envelope.

Sincerely,

Ron S. Diamond   James I. Dermott
President   Chairman of the Board

**Letter Dealing with Financial or
Capital Structure Changes**

• ANNUAL MEETING LETTER

This section offers examples of letters you will need when arranging the annual meeting. They can be used as guides to help you write your own letter, or they can be used as is—all you need to do is insert the appropriate data.

Notice of Annual Meeting of Shareholders

Date _____

    The annual meeting of the shareholders of the _____ Company, for the election of Directors and the transaction of such other business as may properly come before the meeting, will be held at the office of the Company on (day of the week) _____, 19— —, at _____ a.m.

    If you cannot be present at the meeting, please sign and return the accompanying proxy in the enclosed envelope.

                                             _____

                                             Secretary

Call of Regular Annual Meeting of Shareholders by the President

To _____, Secretary:

    Under power given to me by the By-Laws of the _____ Corporation, as President of the _____ Corporation, I hereby call the regular annual meeting of the shareholders of the _____, to be held on (day of the week), _____ 19— —, at _____ a.m., at the principal office of the Corporation, _____ Street, City of _____, State of _____, for the following purposes:

    (1) to elect a board of _____ directors for the ensuing year; (2) to consider and vote upon the approval and ratification of all contracts, acts, proceedings, elections, and appointments which shall have been theretofore made or taken by the Board of Directors, as set forth in the minutes of the meetings of the Board of Directors; and (3) to transact such other business as may properly come before the meeting or any adjournments thereof.

    You are directed, as Secretary of the _____ Corporation, to give notice of the meeting in the manner prescribed in the By-Laws.

    Date at _____, this _____ day of _____, 19— —.

                                               _____

                                             President

STEEL PRODUCTS CORP.

PITTSBURGH, PENNSYLVANIA

Notice of Annual Meeting

To Our Shareholders:

You are cordially invited to attend the annual meeting to be held June 12, 19— —, at 10 a.m. in the Conference Room of the Corporate Building.

The agenda for the meeting includes election of Directors and some corporate changes that are under consideration by the Board.

If you are unable to attend this meeting, please date and sign the enclosed proxy and return it promptly. Unless otherwise instructed, your proxy will be voted in accordance with the judgment of the proxy holders named by you in the proxy.

Thank you.

Yours truly,

John Trevnick
President

Annual Meeting Letter

Shareholder's Proxy for Annual Meeting

_____ Company
Shareholder's Proxy
No _____

Number of Shares
Preferred _____
Common _____

This proxy is solicited by order of the Board of Directors _____,
President, _____, Vice-President, and _____, Secretary, or any
one of them are hereby appointed the proxies of the undersigned, with full
power of substitution to vote and otherwise act for the undersigned at any
annual or special meeting of the shareholders (or members) of the
_____ Company (or Society) or any adjournment or adjournments
thereof, for the election of Directors, and for the transaction of such other
business as may properly come before any such meeting, as fully as the
undersigned could vote and act if personally present.

Date _____   Signed _____

Proxy Follow-Ups

Dear _____:

The proxy form sent to you with the annual report has not been received
by us. A quorum at our annual meeting depends upon proxy returns. A large
number of our shareholders reside at points so far from _____ that
they cannot attend in person. Consequently, the purpose of this notice is to
emphasize the importance of the timely receipt of proxies.

We hope you will attend this year's meeting. If, however, you do not
expect to do so, please sign and mail the proxy. In the event you have mislaid
the previous copy, a duplicate proxy and a self-addressed stamped envelope is
enclosed.

Thank you.

Yours very truly,

_____,
President

Letter Thanking Stockholder for Signed Proxy

Dear _____:

Thank you for sending in your dated and signed proxy for our annual meeting of shareholders.

We especially appreciate your kind remarks about the Company and its employees. Let me assure you that we will continue to do the best job we can in behalf of our shareholders.

Sincerely,

3

Personal Letters Every Executive Must Write

      This chapter presents a working kit of model personal letters that you might want to write. While some letters may be categorized as business obligations, most personal letters are written on your own initiative, expressing a personal sentiment.

      You will find that the letter with a friendly, informal tone will be the one most appreciated. On the other hand, too "chummy" a letter could offend your reader. To find the right degree of informality, ask yourself: Is the person to whom I'm writing an acquaintance or a friend? If the latter, how close a friend? How old is he or she? What is the letter about? The answers will help you decide on the best tone.

      The opportunities for writing a personal letter that distinctly express your feelings are almost infinite. This chapter provides a broad selection of samples to guide you in as many situations as possible.

• LETTER OF CONDOLENCE

A letter of sympathy to someone who lost a relative or friend through death is one of the most difficult letters to write, Moreover, laboring over such a letter can make it sound forced and insincere. A simple, heartfelt message is the kind that will be most appreciated and give the most comfort.

General Rules

Be honest and sincere.

Don't heap compliments upon compliments. That will make the letter stilted, artificial.

Keep the use of "I" to an absolute minimum; keep the focus on the reader.

Keep the letter short.

Alternate Phrases

(a) All of us here at Walker & Co., would like to extend our deepest sympathy on the untimely passing of your president, Mr. Harold Stevens.

The shocking news that your daughter was involved in a fatal accident came to me only a few minutes ago. She was an outstanding person, and I know what a great loss this is for you.

Every member of the Board of Directors joins me in extending to you sincere condolences upon the loss of your husband.

(b) Over the years, we came to look forward to Mr. Stevens's visits. He was a gentleman in the truest sense of the word, and I doubt if there are many men in our industry who possess his depth of knowledge and his high regard for others.

There is little anyone can do or say at a time like this, but I wanted you to know that my thoughts and my deepest sympathy are with you during these trying times.

It's still hard to realize completely that we are to be denied his association—something that we who knew him valued greatly. For all of us it was a great privilege to have known Robert, and we shall miss him very much.

(c) We shall sincerely miss him.

If I can help you in any way, please call on me.

If there is any help or information we can give you, please call me personally.

LINWOOD KNITTING MILLS, INC.

50 HARRISON AVENUE

JOHNSTON, INDIANA

XXXXXXXXXXXXXX
XXXXXXXXXXXXX
XXXXXXXXXXXXX

Dear Mrs. Jones:

I was greatly shocked yesterday to learn of your husband's sudden death. Please accept my sincere condolences.

I met Dave when he joined our company sixteen years ago, and we enjoyed a close and friendly association.

Dave had the respect and admiration of his colleagues, many of whom were his friends as well. His cheerful disposition was an inspiration to all of us. He will be greatly missed by his co-workers and friends here at the company.

If I can be of any help to you, Mrs. Jones, please let me know.

Sincerely yours,

Letter of Condolence

• LETTER EXPRESSING SOLICITUDE

In a letter showing concern over an illness or misfortune, sincerity and tact are the most important qualities. A solicitous letter should carry a feeling of warmth to the recipient. It should also offer some genuine encouragement and help.

General Rules

Keep the letter brief.
Keep the tone of the letter encouraging.
Don't philosophize.
Don't dramatize the illness or misfortune.

Alternate Phrases

(a) Helen told me this morning that you've been down with the mumps for over two weeks. I hope that by the time this reaches you you'll be feeling much better.

At the lodge meeting yesterday, Ron told us how ill Tom has been. I was extremely sorry to hear this; he's such a fine lad.

I can well understand how hard it is to see a modern facility such as yours destroyed by fire. But I know that you, more than anybody, have the perseverance and courage to surmount an unfortunate event like this.

(b) With this note I'm sending along some books I think you'll enjoy. They might help to pass some of those long hours in bed.

Tom's illness must be a terrible strain on you and Mary, but I just know that he'll soon be well again and able to return to school.

Is there anything we here at Scotch Company can do to help you? Please remember that we would be happy to give assistance in any way we can.

(c) Get well soon, and please give my best to your family.

Please give Tom my best, and tell him that my family and I wish him a speedy recovery.

Call me at the office or at home, whichever is more convenient for you.

TRANSATLANTIC AIR CARGO

3900 JUNIPER AVENUE

KINGSTON, NEW YORK

XXXXXXXXXXXXXX
XXXXXXXXXXXXXX
XXXXXXXXXXXXXX

Dear Pete:

Since I had lunch with you only last week, I was truly shocked when I learned this morning that you are in the hospital. However, I was greatly relieved to hear that the operation was successful and you are on your way to complete recovery.

Now I know the hospital is not the most pleasant place to be, but try to rest and take it easy before you get back to work.

In any case, take care of yourself, and if I can do anything or if you need anything, phone me.

Best wishes,

Letter Expressing Solicitude

• LETTER OF CONGRATULATION

Friends and business associates will appreciate a letter congratulating them on some accomplishment or honor.

General Rules

Be prompt; "stale" congratulations lose much of their effect.
Be natural. Don't use stilted phrases.
Inject an enthusiastic note into the letter. It should not sound like a "duty" letter.
Be brief.

Alternate Phrases

(a) The morning papers confirmed what I heard last night on the TV about your decisive victory over your opponent.

I was delighted but not surprised to hear of your promotion. I can't think of anyone better qualified to tackle such a responsible and demanding job.

I know how pleased and proud you must be of your son being voted as "The Most Valuable NFL Football Player of the Year." Of course, being as outstanding a player as he is, he couldn't miss.

I was very happy to learn that you've recently been made a member of Rubinstein et Cie. Your addition to the firm will surely be a great asset.

As a citizen of Scraggy, I'd like to express my sincere thanks and appreciation to you, Mayor Turgess, for the wise and honest leadership you've given our city.

(b) My congratulations and best wishes to you, Senator. I know you will do your best for your constituents and for our country.

Congratulations and best wishes.

Please give Kenneth my congratulations and best wishes for continued success.

My congratulations to you and to the firm. You have my best wishes for success and satisfaction in your new position.

Over the past years our town has become a better place to live, and for that, we as citizens, owe you our thanks.

INVESTMENT INSURANCE CO.

950 QUEENSCOURT AVENUE

STYELING, NEW HAMPSHIRE

XXXXXXXXXXXXXXX
XXXXXXXXXXXXXX
XXXXXXXXXXXXXX

Dear Mr. Waler:

I've just read of your election as president of the Oklahoma Bar Association, and I'd like to extend my warmest congratulations to you on this fine recognition of your ability.

Members of the Bar Association should also be complimented for the splendid choice they've made.

You have my very best wishes for what I know will be a successful term.

Sincerely,

Letter of Congratulation

• MAKING AN APPOINTMENT

These letters fall into two groups: you ask for an appointment, or you ask someone to come to your office.

General Rules

State the purpose of the appointment, but don't go into details unless you have to.

Ideally, suggest the time, place, and the date of the appointment.

Or, ask the person to whom you are writing to suggest these details.

Ask for confirmation of the appointment.

Alternate Phrases

(a) I will be in New York on August 1. I would appreciate it if I could see you and discuss the new fall line with you.

Can you be in my office on September 11, at 9:30 a.m.? I would like to discuss employment with you.

The papers in connection with the trust you are creating for your daughter are now complete, except for your signature. Could you come to my office sometime this week to sign them?

We here at ABC Company are very excited about the new line, and feel that once you see it you will be too.

(b) Will it be convenient for me to call at your office at 10 a.m. on October 3?

Please let me know if this time is convenient for you.

Please phone me when it will be convenient for you to do this.

I would very much like to demonstrate our new word processing system for you. Will it be convenient for you if I call at your office around 10 a.m. on September 7?

(c) (This paragraph may be omitted.)

If another date and time is more convenient for you, please let me know.

I'm sure the time we spend together discussing this subject will be time well spent.

CENTURY ELECTRONIC DEVICES

CENTURY PARK

BROOKS, MASSACHUSETTS

XXXXXXXXXXXXXX
XXXXXXXXXXXXXX
XXXXXXXXXXXXXX

Dear James:

Having just returned from Chicago where I conferred with Robert Greenwood, President of Electromatic Corporation, I believe it would be in the interest of both of us to discuss the various topics that Robert and I talked about.

Please call early next week and let me know when it will be convenient for you to see me.

Sincerely,

Making an Appointment

• HOSPITALITY LETTERS

When someone is hospitable to you, it becomes an excellent occasion to make a good relationship even better by writing the individual a hospitality letter. Unfortunately, many executives, because of heavy schedules and reluctance to compose such a letter, let such a perfect opportunity slip by. The following examples will help you write a hospitality letter without taking too much of your time or your effort.

General Rules

Be grateful for the hospitality extended to you, but don't be mushy.
Be brief and to the point.

Alternate Phrases

(a) Thank you for your hospitality in showing me around your plant. I appreciate it.

It was good of you to take me and my business associates to lunch in order to continue our discussion on the proposed merger between the two companies. Your hospitality is greatly appreciated.

(b) I was quite impressed with both your equipment and the obvious efficiency of your employees.

Because of your generous gesture we have accomplished within one day what we thought would take several days.

(c) You can rest assured that I shall relay my impressions of your operations to Mr. Dwight, our Purchasing Director, who is considering placing an order with you.

Consequently, we are ready for the next step in this complicated process, thanks to you.

CENTURY ELECTRONIC DEVICES

CENTURY PARK

BROOKS, MASSACHUSETTS

XXXXXXXXXXXXXX
XXXXXXXXXXXXXX
XXXXXXXXXXXXXX

Dear _____:

I want to thank you and A.G. Roberts Co. Inc., for your gracious hospitality in allowing me to make a presentation of our desktop-computer color graphics to your Engineering Department.

The response from your staff was most gratifying. Moreover, the questions asked of me after the presentation were challenging as well as meaningful. I couldn't have asked for a better audience.

If you or any of your staff have any additional questions about our desktop-computer color graphics system, please don't hesitate to call me.

Sincerely,

Hospitality Letter

• LETTER OF APOLOGY

When you have an adequate and convincing explanation of a situation that requires an apology, take the time to devote a few words to that explanation. If you don't have a good excuse, it is often best to admit it; frankness can have a disarming effect upon the reader.

General Rules

Try to achieve a tone of warmth and friendliness.
Make your apology in a straightforward manner.
Admit that you were wrong, but don't grovel.

Alternate Phrases

(a) Please accept my apology for not being at the committee meeting yesterday afternoon.

I should have written to you weeks ago, and I apologize for not having done so.

When I wrote on October 1 that you would receive copies of our profit sharing agreement within a few days, I did so with the best of intentions.

I sincerely regret the last-minute postponement of our conference yesterday.

(b) To be quite honest about it, the meeting slipped my mind completely, and I didn't think of it until last night. I am sorry that I wasn't at the committee's first meeting, and I'll do my best to make up for it.

The generous assistance you gave me was a great help, and I fully expected to write you as soon as I returned home. Upon reaching the office, however, an emergency developed and I had to leave immediately for Ohio. Well, I'm back and can now write this long overdue letter.

Naturally, I was embarrassed to discover this morning that the material had not yet been mailed. Please accept my apology for the delay.

A transportation tie-up, however, at our parts plants made it necessary for me to drive over there on a very short notice. I hope you will be generous enough to understand the unavoidable nature of the situation.

(c) (This paragraph may be omitted.)

The help you gave me in March saved me a great deal of time and effort, and I shall not forget it. If I can be of assistance to you in any way, I hope you will give me an opportunity to return your kindness.

The documents are sent to you today under separate cover. They should reach you very shortly. I hope you will find them useful.

If it's convenient for you to come to my office Wednesday or Thursday before noon, I shall be glad to see you and be of assistance to you in any way I can.

A.G. ROBERTS CO.

700 CRESTVIEW AVENUE

DENNIS, ILLINOIS

XXXXXXXXXXXXXX
XXXXXXXXXXXXXX
XXXXXXXXXXXXXX

Dear _____:

In returning your Real Estate Investment Reports, I want to express to you both my thanks and my apologies.

I'm afraid the length of time I have kept this material is nothing short of disgraceful. My study of the reports, however, has been interrupted frequently. and I finished reading them only last night.

It was generous of you to make this information available to me, and I do hope you have not been inconvenienced by the delay in their return.

Sincerely yours,

Letter of Apology

• THANK YOU LETTERS

There are few goodwill-builders as basic as the letter of thanks for a favor or a kind act. Yet, like many busy executives, you may find yourself so rushed that the opportunity slips by and the letter doesn't get written. These examples will help you say "thanks" despite a heavy schedule.

General Rules

Make clear what it is you thank the reader for.
Be sincere in your gratitude, but don't "gush."
Whenever possible, let the reader know the further results of his kind act.

Alternate Phrases

(a) I wish I could tell you how much I appreciate your nice letter.

Robert is up and around now, and the doctor assures us there will be no permanent after-effects from the accident. You can imagine how relieved we were to hear that.

Thank you so much for the impressive set of five books which you sent me.

(b) We're mighty proud to have people like Andy Mack on our team, and we're mighty happy that people like you take the time and trouble to write and tell us about one of our employees.

Your kind letter came at a time when our spirits were very low indeed, and it certainly helped us to take a more hopeful outlook.

It was very thoughtful of you to remember my birthday, and I really appreciate it.

(c) I'm passing your letter along to Andy. I know he'll enjoy reading it as much as I did.

Ann joins me in thanking you sincerely for your concern and good wishes for Robert.

Thanks again for the gift.

(d) (This paragraph may be omitted.)

Thanks again for writing and for giving me a chance to put another letter of recommendation in Andy's personnel file.

We will always be grateful for your thoughtfulness.

I'll be looking forward to our next meeting. Let's make it soon.

BILL BROCK

310 FIRST STREET, SOUTHEAST

WASHINGTON, D.C.

XXXXXXXXXXXXXX
XXXXXXXXXXXXXX
XXXXXXXXXXXXXX

Dear Mr. Muller:

I wanted to write you now, at this very special time of Thanksgiving, to tell you how grateful I am for everything you have done for our Committee.

No organization has ever had a more loyal or more dedicated friend than you, Mr. Muller.

In the four years I've served as Chairman, I've watched our organization regain its strength, its confidence, and its purpose. And I truly believe that you are the one who deserves a good share of the credit.

I know I have written to you many times asking for your help. And whenever you could, you gave and gave generously. For that and more, every member of our Committee owes you a special debt of gratitude.

As you celebrate Thanksgiving with your family and friends, as I will with mine, I'm sure each of us has many things for which we are grateful. But I hold your support of our organization and your friendship as a very special blessing.

Very truly yours,

Bill Brock

Through the courtesy of William E. Brock, U.S. Trade Representative,
Washington, D.C.

Thank You Letters

• LETTER OF INTRODUCTION

You can prepare a letter of introduction to be delivered in person by the one introduced, or you can prepare it for direct mailing to the addressee. If you are going to give it to the one to be introduced, leave it unsealed as a courtesy to him or her. However, the best way, if there is enough time, is to mail the letter directly to the addressee.

General Rules

In addition to the name of the person being introduced, include his or her business affiliation, and the reason for the introduction.

Add personal information if you think it will help break the ice (both persons may be good golfers, or amateur photographers, for instance).

Make it clear that any courtesy shown to the introduced person will be appreciated.

Alternate Phrases

(a)   This letter will introduce you to Alan Barry, a fine engineer, with whom I have had the privilege to work on many projects.

I have just learned that Stacy Gorelick, a good friend of mine, has been transferred by her company, the Amos Computer Company, to Chicago and you will be one of her accounts.

Sometime within the next week, our new Marketing Representative, George Bayles, will call at your office.

(b)   Alan is engaged in road construction at the present time. I thought that since you have had experience in similar and highly successful projects, perhaps you could give him some valuable suggestions. I'm sure that whatever information you can give Alan will help him greatly.

Stacy is one of the most knowledgeable systems engineers in the field, and you can certainly rely on any information she gives you.

You will find George eager to serve your needs in the same reliable and satisfactory way he served his previous customers. We are sure you will like his pleasing personality and competence.

(c)   I will certainly appreciate any help you can give him, and you know, of course, that if ever I can reciprocate I would be most pleased to do so.

If there is anything you can do to help Stacy learn her way around your data processing facility, I would be most appreciative.

We are looking forward to a prosperous year, as I'm sure you are, and I know that George will do his utmost to help make it so for you.

GENERAL HOSPITAL

80 REGENT BOULEVARD

RAMSHEAD, PENNSYLVANIA

XXXXXXXXXXXXXXX
XXXXXXXXXXXXXX
XXXXXXXXXXXXXX

Dear Marsha:

For some time now I have wanted you to meet a very good friend of mine, John Peter, Vice President of Marketing, Kronk Pharmaceutical Company.

John is touring the country to gather information about the effectiveness of his company's products. I'm sure this is an area in which you can be quite valuable to him.

Because I believe that you will not only be able to help each other but will also enjoy each other's company, I'm writing this letter of introduction. I will, of course, appreciate any help you can give John.

Sincerely yours,

Letter of Introduction

• OFFERING A RECOMMENDATION

You should not agree to recommend someone unless you are convinced of the person's qualifications, honesty, and integrity. If you do recommend someone, give the person the honest praise he or she deserves. Remember, though, not to give more praise than is merited. Your reader depends on *your* integrity as a responsible executive not to mislead him or her.

General Rules

Inject an enthusiastic tone into your letter.
Make the letter a personal one.
Give as many facts as you think necessary.

Alternate Phrases

(a) Please accept my recommendation of John Roberts without any reservation.

I'm pleased to send you the information you asked for concerning the record of Marsha Smith.

Paul Bell has been an associate of mine for five years, and it is with great pleasure that I recommend him for the _____ position in your organization.

(b) I have known John for six years, and can unequivocally attest to his enthusiasm, integrity, and ability. I'm certain that when you meet him you will be impressed by his personal charm.

Marsha was employed at our DP center as an Applications Programmer for the past three years. We were quite pleased with her productivity and efficiency. She approached her work as a professional, and communicated well with her superiors and colleagues.

Paul has been active in community affairs for many years, having served as district attorney. He is now devoting much of his time and effort to fight juvenile delinquency. All who know him have the highest regard for him.

(c) I can heartily recommend John, and know he will be a valued addition to your staff.

It is a distinct pleasure to recommend Marsha to you.

There is absolutely no doubt in my mind that Paul will be a valuable asset to your organization.

TRANSPACIFIC AIR FREIGHT

435 MAGNOLIA AVENUE

SOUTH SAN FRANCISCO, CALIFORNIA

XXXXXXXXXXXXXX
XXXXXXXXXXXXXX
XXXXXXXXXXXXXX

Dear Harry:

When we had lunch together a few weeks ago, I mentioned Jack Hunt, a Project Management Consultant, who did such an excellent job for us. Since that time he decided to move to your part of the country, Dallas, Texas.

I don't know whether or not you're interested in project management consulting, but I think Jack can offer you some novel ways in making project management at your facility more cost-efficient and profitable. Moreover, I can assure you of one thing, he really knows his field.

Harry, talk to this fellow. It won't cost you anything, and you just might benefit by it.

Sincerely,

Offering a Recommendation

• INVITING AN EXECUTIVE TO JOIN IN CIVIC PROJECT

Yours may be the job of getting capable men and women to help in a worthwhile community project. It takes a good and convincing letter to persuade an executive with a premium on his or her time to decide that he/she should give some of it to you.

General Rules

> Be specific about the civic project.
> Emphasize the need for such work.
> Stress the qualities the reader has that you need.
> Specifically ask him or her to join.
> Articulate your appreciation if the person's decision will be affirmative.

Alternate Phrases

(a) We all know how tragic the plight is of those stricken with cancer, and we all sympathize with them. Many of us do what we can to help. Yet how many of us can say that we are doing enough?

Each year more and more young people find it impossible to continue their education due to lack of funds. The Young People's College Fund was established ten years ago for the purpose of helping worthwhile youths get into the college of their choice.

Campaign time is approaching, and the _____ Party of Riverdale is forming a committee to help formulate party strategy.

(b) We now need high-caliber executives to help organize a massive fund-raising campaign. We are inviting you and a few others who have the necessary ability and background to help do this job.

But a fund is only as good as the people who administer it. Since decision making is essential in achieving maximum effectiveness from this fund, we need people who are used to and can make responsible decisions.

There are many issues that must be included in the coming campaign, and many decisions have to be made as to how, when, and where to present them. We need knowledgeable, fast-thinking people to help run this show. That is why we are writing to you.

(c) The time you devote to this project will be negligible compared to the satisfaction you will get by knowing your efforts have helped so many unfortunate people. Please say that you will help.

We know you can help. We can only hope you will.

Please join us. We are sure that you will find the work interesting.

PREMIER ELECTRICAL CO.

455 GAINSBORO AVENUE

RALEIGH, NORTH CAROLINA

XXXXXXXXXXXXXX
XXXXXXXXXXXXXX
XXXXXXXXXXXXXX

Dear Ms Stevens:

I am sure that as a good citizen of our community you are aware of, and care about, the tremendously important work being done by the League for Parent Education.

This year we have expanded our operations, and we have undertaken responsibilities never before attempted by any similar group.

We need very badly the talents and abilities of people like yourself with executive background to help run this project. Could you possibly contribute a little of your time to this most worthwhile endeavor? Not only the League but the whole community would be most grateful and appreciative.

Sincerely yours,

Inviting an Executive to Join in Civic Project

• SOLICITING FOR CHARITABLE CONTRIBUTIONS

Many people find writing the solicitation letter a troublesome task. The samples here should help you handle this problem successfully.

General Rules

Name the charity.
Emphasize the satisfaction the reader will derive from his or her contribution.
Convince the reader of the worthiness of the cause.
Tell the person that his/her contribution, whatever the amount, will be used advantageously.

Alternate Phrases

(a) Once a year we at Friendship House send letters to our friends asking for help. And once again you are in a position to help us perform a service so vitally needed by so many unfortunate older citizens.

Help! Help! Help! We really need your help. The work load of Hope Indian School has tripled in the past year due to increased enrollment. As a result, so much more is asked of us.

Give the United Way! You know that we are a valid organization that needs your contribution to help people in dire need.

(b) These impoverished, lonely old people need a place they can call a home. Think of what your contribution can mean to them. Think of the satisfaction you will get knowing that you have done your share to help these poor old folks.

We willingly take on the added responsibilities, but we ask our friends to aid us by contributing a little of their money to this cause.

Think of the wonderfully good feeling you will get by helping sick and needy people through your contribution.

(c) Please send us a contribution. Whatever amount you can give will be used most beneficially.

Won't you use the enclosed envelope to send us your contribution? Any amount you send will be greatly appreciated.

The small contribution is as welcome as the large one. So whatever you can afford, please send it now. Thank you so much.

ANIMALS HAVE RIGHTS, TOO, Inc.

ASTORIA, L.I., N.Y.

WILL YOU JOIN IN OUR FIGHT?

That's right, we're asking you to join us in our fight AGAINST the abuse, wasteful proliferation, and slaughter of pets, and FOR the rights of animals.

These rights include: care and feeding, spaying or neutering, and proper veterinary's attention, when necessary.

The tools we're using in our battle are: educating adults through the various media; educating children through lectures and posters in schools and libraries; and providing a free spaying and neutering clinic.

But we can't fight alone. WE NEED YOU! The abused and abandoned animals NEED YOU!

Please, right now, will you make out a check for as much as you can afford and mail it in the self-addressed envelope?

We will appreciate it! The poor animals you rescue from slaughter will appreciate it!

Sincerely,

Soliciting for Charitable Contributions

• REFUSAL TO LEND NAME TO FUND-RAISING DRIVE OR CHARITABLE ORGANIZATION

Being asked to contribute the prestige of your name to a fund-raising campaign or a charitable organization is an honor. You may, however, have a number of good reasons for turning down such a request.

General Rules

Give the letter a gracious tone.
Give a straightforward reason for your refusal.
Praise the cause for which the drive is being held.
Extend your best wishes for the success of the drive.

Alternate Phrases

(a) It is with regret that I decline your request for the use of my name for so worthy a cause as the Protect the Whales Fund.

I am very sorry that I cannot grant you permission to use my name in your fund-raising drive for the Non-Alcoholic Drive Fund.

Please be assured that I would be most happy to lend my name to your fund-raising drive on behalf of the World Wildlife Fund. Unfortunately, however, I cannot.

(b) You see, I am personally involved in working with the Cancer Fund, and want to concentrate my effort on their behalf. I wouldn't want my name to be used by any organization unless I can actively participate in it.

Through the years I have permitted my name to be used by any group that seemingly had a good cause. Unfortunately, some groups were irresponsible in their use of my name. Because of these past unpleasant occurrences, I no longer permit the use of my name by anyone.

I have already given permission to a number of groups to use my name, and for this year at least, that is all I can agree to.

(c) I know you will understand my feelings in the matter. Perhaps at a future time I will be in a better position to grant your request. In the meantime, best wishes for a successful fund-raising drive.

Nevertheless, I do wish you the best success in your drive.

Do write me the next time you have a fund-raising drive. I may then be in a position to give you my permission to use my name. Best wishes for a huge success.

APEX REALTY COMPANY

445 CARRIAGE HILL ROAD

TARRYVILLE, VERMONT

XXXXXXXXXXXXXXX
XXXXXXXXXXXXXX
XXXXXXXXXXXXXX

Dear Mr. Beson:

Regretfully, I can't comply with your request to use my name in your fund-raising drive.

I have allowed my name to be used for this purpose by a number of non-profit organizations, and whatever beneficial effect it could have has already been diluted to a great extent. Consequently, as a matter of policy, and even though the Cancer Fund is a most worthy cause, I'm limiting the use of my name to those groups already using it.

Nonetheless, I wish you great success in your drive.

Sincerely,

Refusal to Lend Name to Fund-Raising Drive

• ACCEPTING MEMBERSHIP IN PROFESSIONAL
OR SERVICE ORGANIZATION

If you decide to accept the honor of membership in a professional or service organization, here are sample letters to help you handle this pleasant job.

General Rules

Be prompt in your response.
Be warm and friendly, but businesslike.

Alternate Phrases

(a)   Your cordial invitation asking me to join the Lions Club is very flattering, and I accept with great pleasure.

I appreciate your letter of June 14, expressing your desire to have me join the American Business Women Association.

Thank you for your letter of October 10. It was very nice of you to invite me to join the Olympic Athletic Club.

(b)   I consider it an honor to become a member of the Lions Club, and I intend to share in the efforts of all your members to try to achieve your worthy goals.

I accept with great pleasure your invitation. Please be assured that I intend to participate in all the responsibilities entailed in that membership.

I have always admired the work you have done, and I now accept your invitation with great pleasure.

(c)   Please convey my thanks to the other members for this invitation. I look forward to seeing you at the next meeting.

Thanks again for your invitation. I'm looking forward to meeting members of the local chapter of the ABWA at the next meeting.

If I can be of any help before the next meeting, please call upon me.

A.G. ROBERTS CO

700 CRESTVIEW AVENUE

DENNIS, ILLINOIS

XXXXXXXXXXXXXX
XXXXXXXXXXXXXX
XXXXXXXXXXXXXX

Dear Ms Green:

Thank you for your letter inviting me to become a member of the American Advertising Executives Association.

I will be happy to join such a group of outstanding executives, and welcome the chance to participate in the worthwhile activities of your well-known association.

I look forward to meeting you and your colleagues, and to thanking you all personally.

Sincerely,

**Accepting Membership in Professional
or Service Organization**

• LETTER OF RESIGNATION FROM ORGANIZATION

When it becomes necessary to resign your membership in an organization, for whatever reason, you should put it in writing. A letter of resignation should be direct and sincere. Even though you may be resigning in protest, it should not be unpleasant in tone.

General Rules

Be direct; state briefly why you are resigning.
Avoid accusations or recriminations.
Include a complimentary comment, if possible.

Alternate Phrases

(a) I am very sorry to tell you that because of added job responsibilities I have to resign from the Professional Club.

Please accept my resignation from the Real Estate Planning Board.

I'm reluctantly submitting my resignation, to take effect December 1.

(b) As you know, I was promoted to Vice President of Purchasing, and since then I have very little time for anything but my work.

The policies recently adopted by the Executive Committee are highly unsatisfactory to me. I do not care to remain a member of the Board.

My association with the Travelers has generally been a good one. However, I have become involved with another organization that is more compatible with my professional interests.

(c) I will miss the Club and all the friends I have made there. But perhaps when my situation changes, I will again be in a position to join you.

Nevertheless, I leave with the highest regard for you and the Board's goals.

I appreciate our long and pleasant association, and I wish you and the organization the best of luck for continued success.

B.J. FRANKLING PUBLISHING COMPANY

200 SPENCER AVENUE

TALSMUTH, MAINE

XXXXXXXXXXXXXXX
XXXXXXXXXXXXXX
XXXXXXXXXXXXXX

Dear Mr. Sidney:

It is with sincere regret that I resign my membership in the Tennis and Beach Club. My firm has transferred me to their Midwestern territory, and consequently I have to relocate in Chicago.

Please express my appreciation to the Board of Directors for the many courtesies they have shown to me and my family.

I am sorry to have to leave the club and all the members with whom I have had the most cordial relationships, but relocating every few years is an occupational hazard that I accept.

Yours very truly,

Letter of Resignation from Organization

• INFORMAL INVITATION

The informal letter of invitation can also be an effective instrument for getting goodwill. When you write a letter of this type, do it with this goal in mind.

General Rules

Give the letter a cordial and gracious tone.

Include details, such as when and where the particular event will take place. Base the degree of informality on the kind of relationship you have with the reader.

Alternate Phrases

(a) The Cross-Country Corporation will have a table at the annual meeting of the Trucking Association at the Hilton Hotel at 7:30 p.m. on February 10. We cordially invite you to be our guest at the dinner.

I was very happy to learn recently that you are going to be in Chicago next week. Could we possibly get together on Thursday?

I was glad to read in your letter of May 6 that you will be in San Francisco next month. It will be good to see you again.

(b) Before dinner we could have cocktails in the Tropic Lounge, after which dinner will be served in the Edgewood Room.

We could meet at my office around 11:30 or so, and then walk to the best little restaurant in town for lunch.

I hope that you haven't made other plans, because my wife and I would be happy to have you as our house guest during your stay in town.

(c) We hope you can accept our invitation and come to this annual affair which promises to be interesting and entertaining. Please let us know.

I look forward to another informative and interesting discussion with you.

If you can accept our invitation, please drop me a line.

CENTURY ELECTRONIC DEVICES

CENTURY PARK

BROOKS, MASSACHUSETTS

XXXXXXXXXXXXXX
XXXXXXXXXXXXXX
XXXXXXXXXXXXXX

Dear Jerry:

On Thursday, December 4, the local chapter of Data Processing Management Association in joint endeavor with the Institute of Electrical and Electronics Engineers, is putting on a computer fair in the Green Room of the Plaza Hotel to which I would like to invite you as my personal guest.

The affair will start at 5:30 p.m. and will include six mini- and microcomputer vendors demonstrating at least ten products and several software packages. We will also have Ross Glazer from the National Association for Computing Machinery speaking after dinner.

Please let me know if you can make it. I really think you would enjoy the computer fair, the smorgasboard dinner, and the nationally known speaker.

Sincerely,

Informal Invitation

• ACCEPTING INFORMAL INVITATION

Accepting an invitation in writing should present no problem; the circumstances are pleasant and the letter is straightforward.

General Rules

A short note of thanks is usually sufficient.
Show that you are appreciative of the invitation; be warm and enthusiastic.
Confirm the time and place of the meeting.

Alternate Phrases

(a) I shall be delighted to be your guest at the association's annual dinner meeting in the Hilton Hotel on September 7. Frankly, I had hoped you would invite me; I always wanted to be present at one of Dr. Lee's speeches.

I shall be very glad to have dinner with you when I come to Miami on the 23rd.

Your welcome letter came this morning, inviting me to stay with you during my visit to San Francisco. Of course, I accept with pleasure.

(b) As you suggest, we could meet in the bar around 6:30 so as to give us time to talk a bit before the scheduled dinner and Dr. Lee's presentation.

Meeting you at The Brass Rail is an excellent idea, and I shall be looking forward to it.

It is very generous of you and Mrs. Harris to offer me the hospitality of your home. I appreciate it.

(c) Thanks so much for asking me.

Thanks a lot for thinking of me.

Thank you for inviting me.

NATIONAL CITY BANK

ARLINGTON STREET

BOSTON, MASSACHUSETTS

XXXXXXXXXXXXXXX
XXXXXXXXXXXXXX
XXXXXXXXXXXXXX

Dear Bill:

It was nice of you to invite me to the computer fair to be held on December 4, and I accept with pleasure. The agenda for the evening sounds interesting, besides I'm looking forward to seeing you again.

I plan to get there before 5:30. I don't want to miss any of the demonstrations put on by the mini- and microcomputer vendors.

Thank you very much for the invitation.

Sincerely,

Accepting Informal Invitation

• DECLINING INFORMAL INVITATION

In turning down a friendly invitation, one of your main concerns is to avoid giving offense.

General Rules

Reply promptly; don't put the letter off.
Use as much tact as you can; include a sincere "thank you" for the invitation.
Give the reason why you can't accept.

Alternate Phrases

(a) I was hoping that you would have your Professional Management Seminar sometime in August so that I could attend.

Thank you so much for your generous invitation to spend a few days in your home. I only wish that my itinerary would permit me to do so.

Thank you for your letter of January 9 in which you invited me to attend the conference on real estate financing.

(b) Unfortunately, however, January 9 is a date on which I will be at a meeting in Dallas.

I am only pausing in Denver long enough to make one important call at our largest account. Immediately after, I must be on my way to Los Angeles, where I am scheduled to speak.

Business commitments in New York, however, will make it impossible for me to attend. I would certainly prefer accepting your invitation with thanks, but I have no choice. Regretfully, I have to decline.

(c) Thanks for your invitation. I am sure you will have a very successful seminar.

I really appreciate your invitation. Thanks again.

I do hope that I will be able to attend your next meeting.

LINWOOD KNITTING MILLS, INC

50 HARRISON AVENUE

JOHNSTON, INDIANA

XXXXXXXXXXXXXX
XXXXXXXXXXXXX
XXXXXXXXXXXXXX

Dear Jim:

It was generous of you to invite me in your letter of March 2 to have lunch with you on the 8th, and I appreciate it.

A couple of days ago, however, I agreed to speak before the League of Women Voters at a luncheon to be held on March 8. I'm truly sorry that I have to forego seeing you.

Thank you again for your thoughtfulness. Perhaps we shall be able to get together for lunch at some future date.

Sincerely,

Declining Informal Invitation

• FORMAL INVITATION

There are three basic types of formal invitations:

1. engraved for the occasion
2. partially engraved
3. handwritten

Engraved invitation

For engraved invitations, use black engraving on heavy white or light cream paper with a kid finish. There should be no address, monogram, or initial on the paper. If a coat-of-arms is used, it should be embossed on the paper without colors. The invitation of traditional size requires folding before it is inserted in the envelope, but the modern 4″ by 5½″ invitation is inserted in the envelope without folding.

Partially engraved

A stiff white or ivory card, about 3½″ by 5″, is usually used for partially engraved invitations. However, the invitation may be engraved on the same kind of paper that is used for fully engraved invitations.

Many people who entertain frequently use partially engraved invitations when the number of guests is too small to justify engraving invitations especially for the occasion. Spaces are left for the name of the guest, the nature of the entertainment, the time and the date. People who entertain frequently with small dinners of 20 or more guests also engrave the fourth line, leaving only the name of the guest, the date, and time to be filled in.

If the entertainment is in honor of someone, "in honor of_____" may be inserted after the nature of the entertainment, if space permits. If there is not sufficient space for the additional wording, as is usually the case, "To meet _____" may be written across the top of the invitation above the host's name.

Handwritten formal invitation

Handwritten invitations are used when the number of guests to be invited does not justify engraved invitations. Use heavy white or cream personal writing paper, with engraved address or initials for men, or a monogram for women. If the address is engraved at the top of the stationery, it is not repeated in the invitation. If initialed stationery is used, the address is written below the date and hour. The invitations should be written in script. The wording and spacing are the same as on a partially engraved invitation. When there is a guest of honor, the words "to meet _____" are added after the nature of the entertainment. The words "in honor of" are used only on engraved invitations.

Frederick L. Bebe
requests the pleasure of
Judge Sands
company at a dinner
in honor of
The Right Honorable
Lester B. Pearson

on Friday, the twenty-fifth of March
at seven o'clock
Oval Room
Ritz-Carlton
New York

R.s.v.p.
10 Rockefeller Plaza
Black Tie

Engraved Invitation

Partially Engraved

Mr. and Mrs. Edgar R. Jones

request the pleasure of

Mr. Robertson's

company at dinner

on Tuesday, the eighteenth of June

at half past seven o'clock

550 Park Avenue

Mr. and Mrs. Edgar R. Smith
request the pleasure of
Mr. Robertson's
company at dinner
on Tuesday, the eighteenth of June
at half past seven o'clock
550 Park Avenue

Handwritten Formal Invitation

• ACCEPTING OR DECLINING FORMAL INVITATION

Always answer invitations promptly. Answer them in the same form line by line in which they are issued. A formal invitation in the third person is answered in the third person. If a person particularly regrets having to decline an invitation, he may also write a letter, but this is in addition to the formal regret. Formal answers are written by hand, in script, on personal writing paper. Writing paper with a business letterhead may be used to answer invitations to business luncheons, dinners, or receptions when they have been sent to the office.

Names

Those who send formal invitations identify themselves fully, on the assumption that there might be others by the same name. Only the last name of the guest is used, on the assumption that further identification is unnecessary. The same rule applies when answering an invitation: the person answering writes his own name in full but omits the Christian name of the person sending the invitation. Of course, the full name is used on the envelope.

If the invitation is issued in the name of more than one person, mention each name in the answer.

Wording

In a regret, use the expression "very kind invitation" instead of "kind invitation." Specify the date and hour in an acceptance, but only the date in a regret. The year is not given in an invitation or in an answer.

Abbreviations

The only abbreviations used in a formal invitation are Mr., Mrs., Ms and Dr. The word *junior*, beginning with a small letter, is usually written out.

The hour

The correct form for noting the hour in a formal invitation is "half past eight o'clock" or "half after eight o'clock,"—never "eight-thirty." If the invitation is for a quarter hour, which is unusual, the correct form is "at quarter past eight" or "at quarter before eight."

Excuses

It is unnecessary to state the reason for regretting a formal invitation unless it is issued by The White House or royalty.

Titles

Courtesy titles, such as *Excellency* and *Honorable*, are never used by the holder in issuing or answering invitations. Senators and judges refer to themselves as *Mr.*

900 Park Avenue

Mr Lawrence M Sand
accepts with pleasure
the kind invitation
of
Mr Bebe
to be present at dinner
in honor of
The Right Honorable
Lester B Pearson
on Friday, the twenty fifth of March
at seven o'clock
Oval Room
Ritz - Carlton
New York

Accepting or Declining Formal Invitation

22 EAST 71 STREET

Mr Ralph N Simmons
regrets that he will be unable
to accept the very kind invitation of
Mr Bebe
to attend a dinner
in honor of
The Right Honorable
Lester B Pearson
on Friday the twenty fifth of March

4

Tactful Letters for Promoting Effective Customer Relations

Regardless of the type of industry the executive works in, the alert business person doesn't miss any opportunity to promote customer relations.

For example, the holiday season at the end of the year is an ideal opportunity to strengthen friendship through a note of seasonal greeting. Like the letter of "thank you" to bread-and-butter customers or clients, it should omit any sales message. The letter that best reflects a genuine spirit of friendship and consideration is a natural, informal note written to an individual.

There are many situations covered by the letters in this chapter, including welcoming new customers or clients, apologizing for action of an employee, computer error, or faulty merchandise, and acknowledging receipt of queries or complaints. All you need to use is one or two of them with any one of your customers to let the person know you value his or her patronage.

• WELCOMING POTENTIAL CLIENT/CUSTOMER TO TOWN

Because a letter of welcome is a courteous and friendly gesture, in addition to being just good business, the investment of just a few minutes of your time can reap long-range benefits.

General Rules

Make your letter warm and friendly.
Make it a sales letter, but avoid even the suggestion of high pressure.
Include a sincere invitation to visit your place of business.

Alternate Phrases

(a) Welcome to Lancaster! We are certain that you will like living here, and we, at Lancaster Interior Decorating, will do everything in our power to help you feel at home.

 We just learned that at the beginning of this month you became a resident of Gainesville. It is a great pleasure to welcome you to our beautiful city and certainly to our store.

 The Madison Chamber of Commerce extends to you a most hearty welcome. We are sure you will like it here, and we hope you will call upon us if we can be of any service to you.

(b) You are cordially invited to visit with us as soon as it is convenient for you. Our friendly and helpful personnel will be happy to show you around our display rooms.

 You will enjoy browsing in our well-stocked and cosmopolitan departments. Because we are confident that we can satisfy your requirements, we are enclosing a charge account application for your convenience.

 As a gesture of goodwill we are sending you a small green plant to help just a little in brightening things up for you during these unsettling days of relocation.

(c) We would appreciate it if you would let us have the opportunity to show you our quality merchandise and to service you.

 We are looking forward to your visit in the near future. You won't be disappointed.

 If there is anything we can do, please don't hesitate to call upon us.

FIRST NATIONAL BANK

WAYCROSS, GEORGIA

XXXXXXXXXXXXXX
XXXXXXXXXXXXXX
XXXXXXXXXXXXXX

Dear _____ :

I would like to take this opportunity to welcome you and the Micro Electronics Corporation to Waycross, and to extend to you a warm and cordial invitation to do your banking with the First National Bank.

Our bank is equipped and staffed to provide you with the most modern banking services available. These include computer-processed payroll services; online video display terminals that connect to our data base management/telecommunication systems so that the tellers can attend to your transactions anywhere in the country quickly and efficiently; a 24-hour, automatic electronic pay-teller (the only one in our city); safety deposit booths; private conference rooms; and a nearby parking lot for your convenience.

We would greatly appreciate the opportunity of serving you and your operation, and we hope that you will come by and see us at an early date.

Cordially yours,

President
DSJ:or

Welcoming Potential Client/Customer to Town

• WELCOMING NEW CLIENTS/CUSTOMERS

The little effort and cost involved in sending a letter of welcome and appreciation to a new client/customer is well repaid. The letter shows the person that his or her account/order has been noted, and has merited individual attention. It should also assure the person that he or she made the right decision, and that your organization can meet his or her requirements.

General Rules

Sincerely thank the individual for his or her account/order.

Briefly describe some of the benefits he or she will derive from doing business with your company. Use this letter to ask for any further information, if necessary.

Alternate Phrases

(a) It is indeed a pleasure to welcome you as a new customer of Fulton Company. We shall try very hard to keep you a satisfied customer.

I want to welcome you and Boyington, Inc., in joining the other distinguished corporations whose banking needs we have been serving for many years. I also would like to take this opportunity to express our sincere appreciation for establishing an account with us.

Welcoming you as a new client of Berns, Berns, & Sedlick, Attorneys at Law, is a great pleasure for me.

(b) We firmly believe that giving our valued customers something extra in the way of service and quality will insure a long and pleasant association.

However, as we are sure you realize, it is most important that we receive at the earliest possible date your financial data, including payroll, so that your file can be complete and up-to-date.

We will do our best to fulfill our obligation to you by representing your position in any and all cases.

(c) We thank you for your first order, and hope you will accept our invitation to visit our plant at your convenience.

Thank you for the privilege you have given us to service your account.

We are looking forward to serving you in every way possible.

THE EQUITABLE LIFE ASSURANCE SOCIETY OF THE UNITED STATES

1285 AVENUE OF THE AMERICAS

NEW YORK, N.Y.

XXXXXXXXXXXXXX
XXXXXXXXXXXXX
XXXXXXXXXXXXX

Dear _____ :

One of the business duties which I enjoy most is the privilege of welcoming new Equitable policyholders. I want you to know that you have joined a large group of individuals who are dedicated to serve the needs of each one of our millions of policyholders efficiently, courteously, and promptly, while safeguarding the future for all.

Our Agency and Cashiers' offices throughout the country are staffed by thoroughly trained, capable men and women whose first concern is to serve you well. They maintain complete policy records on confidential computer files, and help you and your Equitable agent keep your insurance coverage adequate and economical. They will assist you, for example, in beneficiary changes, policy loans, or other matters which may arise because of a change in your family or in your economic status.

You can be assured that the Equitable investment organization safeguards your savings as a sacred trust, and prudently invests the policyholders' funds in safe and diverse investments.

Since it is impossible for me to meet all of our policyholders, I hope you will accept this note as a personal and cordial greeting to you individually.

Sincerely yours,

President
JFG:ak

Welcoming New Customers

• ACKNOWLEDGING RECEIPT OF LETTER

A very simple way of extending a little courtesy to a customer/client is to write him or her a brief note acknowledging receipt of a letter that can't be answered immediately. Then, if there is any delay in action on the letter, be it a complaint, query, or whatever, the person will know that he or she is not being ignored.

General Rules

Identify the letter you received.

State the action taken in response to the letter.

Give the reason why a note of acknowledgment is sent instead of a complete answer.

Be brief but not curt.

Alternate Phrases

(a) We received your letter of January 21, addressed to Dr. John D. Douglas.

Just a brief note to acknowledge receipt of your letter of March 21.

Due to some unexplainable delay, I received your letter of October 1 only this morning.

(b) We are sorry to have to tell you that Dr. Douglas died January 10. We know that this news will come as a shock to you because you had a long-standing business relationship with him. As yet Dr. Douglas has not been replaced.

We are forwarding your letter to Ms Karen T. Jackson, who is best equipped to give you the information you need. Ms Jackson is presently at a convention, so her reply will be delayed.

It will take a few days to gather the material you ask for, but I can assure you that it will be sent to you as soon as possible.

(c) Just as soon as a new person is appointed to fill Dr. Douglas's position, I will call his or her attention to your letter.

You can rest assured, however, that as soon as she returns she will answer your letter promptly.

Thank you for thinking of us, and if we can be of any further help, please feel free to call upon us.

NATIONWIDE HOTEL CORP.

800 REGENT BOULEVARD

RAMSHEAD, PENNSYLVANIA

XXXXXXXXXXXXXX
XXXXXXXXXXXXXX
XXXXXXXXXXXXXX

Dear Ms Moss:

Thank you for your letter of June 24 to Mr. Victor R. Verdi. Because of the nature of the letter, it has been forwarded to Ms Diane Foster, Manager of Customer Relations.

Ms Foster will be in touch with you as soon as she returns from a conference in Hawaii.

Sincerely,

Secretary to
Diane Foster

Acknowledging Receipt of Letter

• ADJUSTMENT—WHEN THE ANSWER IS "YES"

A simple letter agreeing with the customer's stand and offering to make amends can do an outstanding job of retaining good customer relationship.

General Rules

Agree with the letter writer graciously; a begrudging tone will nullify the attempt to gain goodwill
Don't be over-apologetic.
Explain clearly what you are doing about the problem.
Mention the unlikelihood of a similar mistake happening again.

Alternate Phrases

(a) We are very pleased that you have given us this opportunity to restore your faith in our product. Rest assured that your selection of our product was no mistake.

It is beyond comprehension how your living room draperies could have been finished so far off the measurements. The man who did the work has been in custom draperies for ten years.

We are very sorry to hear about the experience you had recently. I can't tell you how distressing it is to learn that foreign matter can get and has in fact gotten into our food.

(b) This very morning we have sent you a brand new set, one that has been double and triple checked for defects. You might be interested to know that all our sets are checked in this manner. However, we are only human and sometimes a bad one slips by.

We are not even going to try to alter your bedroom draperies. Since we still have the same material in stock, a new pair of draperies, cut exactly to the measures of your bedroom windows, is in the works already. When the correct draperies are delivered and hung, please give the delivery people the incorrectly cut draperies.

If you could see the precautions that are taken to see that even the smallest impurity does not get into our food, you would be as puzzled as we are to understand how this could happen, as it obviously did in your case.

(c) I am sure you understand. Again, thank you for your patronage, and we certainly hope that the new set will afford you many happy hours of listening.

Please accept my apology for the inconvenience we have caused you.

We are sending you two packages of *Creamer* that we are sure you will find satisfactory. We also want to tell you how sorry we are that you had such an unpleasant experience.

K.B. DOLL CORPORATION

346 CARROLL STREET

BROOKLYN, N.Y.

XXXXXXXXXXXXXXX
XXXXXXXXXXXXXX
XXXXXXXXXXXXXX

Dear Mrs. Bernice Arthur:

Thank you for your understanding letter of November 30 reporting that one of the two dolls you ordered was broken when the package arrived. I cannot blame you at all for being disappointed and even frustrated.

I am sorry that you have been put to so much trouble, but another doll is being sent to you today. I certainly hope that this one arrives intact.

We have modified our packaging, and are confident that we have eliminated the possible cause of breakage. Again, please accept my apology.

Sincerely yours,

Adjustment—When the Answer Is "Yes"

• ADJUSTMENT—WHEN THE ANSWER IS "NO"

The purpose of this letter is not only to deny the customer's request, but also to keep his goodwill while doing so.

General Rules

Be as diplomatic and tactful as possible.
Express understanding of the customer's position.
Explain your position simply and clearly.

Alternate Phrases

(a) We regret to learn from your letter of September 1, that the walnut table you ordered arrived badly damaged.

I was sorry to hear that the printer you purchased from us recently is broken. As soon as we examined the returned printer here in our shop, we determined that the damage was caused by a very heavy object that hit the printer wheel. This opinion has now been confirmed by two outside experts. We are, therefore, not liable for this damage under the guarantee.

The defective electric frying pan which you returned appears to have been submerged in water. This type of pan is not designed to withstand submersion. Unfortunately, you were probably not aware of this. We try to tell our customers about this in the instruction booklet, but sometimes it is overlooked.

(b) Checking our records we found that the railroad company signed a receipt in which they admit receiving the table crated and in perfect condition. Since this is the case, we are afraid that you will have to deal directly with the railroad company to get compensation for the walnut table broken in transit.

Please let us know if you want us to repair the printer and send you the bill, or if you want us to return the broken printer to you.

However, we will be happy to repair the pan for only $8.95; it will then be as good as new.

(c) Thank you for writing, and we hope that this matter will be adjusted to your satisfaction.

I hope that in the future you will be able to protect your printer from being hit by heavy objects.

Please write and tell us if this course of action meets with your approval.

A.G. ROBERTS & COMPANY

700 CRESTVIEW AVENUE

DENNIS, ILLINOIS

XXXXXXXXXXXXXX
XXXXXXXXXXXXXX
XXXXXXXXXXXXXX

Dear Mr. Cranford:

We are sorry to learn that you are having trouble with your six-year-old Perfect Refrigerator, and we are confident that your nearest Perfect Appliances dealer can and will remedy the stated condition.

I am sure you will agree that there must be a limit to how long our guarantee can reasonably be honored. Considering the length of time involved in your case, I am afraid that we cannot accept the responsibility for this repair.

Sincerely yours,

Adjustment—When the Answer Is "No"

• THANKS FOR COMPLIMENT TO EMPLOYEE

This is one letter that can cement good customer relations for your company, and it is a pleasure to write. A customer or client who has taken the trouble to write complimenting someone in your company will certainly appreciate your taking the trouble to answer.

General Rules

Make it an appreciative, personal letter.
Be sure to mention names, so the reader will know the employee was properly recognized.
Include a friendly bid for future business.

Alternate Phrases

(a)   It was very nice of you to take the time to write me about the exchange with the Dallas News about California wine.

Many thanks for your letter of March 10, regarding the performance of Captain Jordan Martin while in command of Flight 297 from Binghamton to Pittsburgh recently. We at TWA are quite proud of our staff of pilots, and we feel that our training program is one of the best offered in the industry.

Thank you for writing about the fine job done by our systems engineer, Ms Ann Gross, in finding and remedying the trouble when all the systems crashed recently at your computer center. Letters such as yours are most welcome. They give us an opportunity to commend an employee for excellent performance, and they indicate some success in our efforts to please our valued customers.

(b)   I am sending your letter along to Mr. Fred Beach, president of the Valley Wine Company, in order that he might write you directly with respect to the availability of wine racks in the Dallas area. You will undoubtedly hear from him shortly.

I am sure Captain Martin and his supervisor will appreciate your thoughtfulness in writing regarding the incident outlined in your letter.

I am forwarding a copy of your letter to the appropriate supervisory personnel for their commendation. Both Ms Gross and her superiors will enjoy seeing your letter.

(c)   Again, many thanks for the courtesy of your letter.

Many thanks for your courtesy and your interest.

We hope that you will always find our service satisfactory.

TRANS WORLD AIRLINES, INC.

380 MADISON AVENUE

NEW YORK, N.Y.

XXXXXXXXXXXXXX
XXXXXXXXXXXXXX
XXXXXXXXXXXXXX

Dear Mr. Nemeth:

Thank you very much for your kind letter of April 16 commending Ms Donna Jones, one of our flight attendants.

It is always gratifying to receive a letter such as yours which indicates that our efforts to instill in our personnel a spirit of courtesy and helpfulness have been successful. You may be sure that Ms Jones will receive appropriate recognition and commendation from her immediate superiors, as well as my own thanks and congratulations on a job well done.

Your selection of TWA is very much appreciated, and all of us here eagerly look forward to the privilege of extending to you a cordial welcome aboard our flights in the future. Needless to say, I trust that you will always find the services of all TWA personnel satisfactory in every respect.

Thank you again for your courtesy in writing to me.

Sincerely,

Thanks for Compliment to Employee

• APOLOGY FOR ACTION OF EMPLOYEE

This is an important letter; it can make the difference between the permanent loss of a customer or client and the reinstatement of good customer relations.

General Rules

Thank the customer for his or her letter.
Mention the specific action for which you are apologizing.
State the action you are taking concerning the offending employee.
Express your desire for the customer's continued patronage.

Alternate Phrases

(a) Thank you for your letter of May 17 calling our attention to the incident in one of our restaurants in the city on May 15.

We certainly appreciate your letter of September 2 telling us about the unfortunate experience you had in our store. Please accept our apologies for the rudeness of one of our salesmen.

Many thanks for your letter calling my attention to the actions of one of my employees. Please accept my apologies for the embarrassment caused you at the time.

(b) We are referring your complaint to our national director of customer relations, Mrs. R. Condon, who will investigate the incident and take appropriate corrective action.

Your letter has been forwarded, together with some of my own comments, to the proper department head for further action. I can assure you that no customer will ever again be subjected to this type of experience.

Mr. Kraven has been severely reprimanded for his actions. We have impressed upon him that this type of conduct will not be tolerated by us.

(c) We value all our customers, and it is our policy to provide the highest quality food with the best possible service. Whenever an employee does not meet our high standards, we like to know about it so that steps may be taken to preclude recurrence. We hope that this incident will not stop you from giving the WHITE SWAN restaurants the opportunity to continue to serve you.

We are grateful for your patronage and feel sure that you will have no cause for complaint in the future.

Again, let me apologize for this particular employee's discourtesy, and I sincerely hope that you will visit us again soon.

VALUED MORTGAGE COMPANY

PHOENIX, ARIZONA

Charles C. Goldman
Customer Relations Manager

XXXXXXXXXXXXXX
XXXXXXXXXXXXXX
XXXXXXXXXXXXXX

Dear Ms Rankin:

Thank you for your recent letter. We are sorry to learn about the circumstances which made it necessary for you to write us, and we apologize for the incident.

We agree with you, it's one thing to have a computer error occur, but it's another thing to have the data processing personnel responsible for the error ignore your letters to remedy the situation.

To insure prompt handling, I am referring your letter to Mr. Landos, our data processing department manager. You may expect to hear from him shortly.

You may be sure that we will do our best to resolve any problems our customers may have in a prompt and fair manner.

Thank you for taking the time to bring this matter to our attention.

Sincerely,

Apology for Action of Employee

• LETTER OF APOLOGY (GENERAL)

Customers will write to you complaining about real or imagined offenses. If you believe the complaint to be justified, tell the writer so and gracefully apologize. If you determine that the complaint is not justified, thank the writer for pointing out the "offense," and gracefully apologize even if no apology is due. After all, it does no harm to the image of your company to say, "We are sorry."

General Rules

Thank the writer for his or her time and effort to write you.

If possible, explain how the incident occurred. Make it clear that such incidents do not occur very often.

If practicable, offer a small token gift or free service to soothe his or her irritated feelings.

Alternate Phrases

(a) Thank you for your recent letter, bringing to our attention the deficiencies in the cutting ability of our gas lawnmower, *Zip II*.

Thank you for taking the time to write us. Let me assure you that the management of Aco Paper Company is most interested in and concerned about your satisfaction.

Thank you for your letter of July 1, in which you point out the inefficient labeling on our Hawaiian products. It is this type of constructive criticism that has helped us attain the general high degree of proficiency we are noted for.

(b) I am sorry that you had such an unfortunate experience with our gas lawnmower, and you will be glad to know that just last week one of our engineers came up with an idea to eliminate this type of situation.

I am sorry that you have been inconvenienced to the extent indicated in your letter. We can assure you that yours is a rare experience, as our company takes every precaution to avoid such occurrences.

We are sorry for the bothersome experience you had, and be assured that we will do everything in our power to keep it from happening again.

(c) Because we value your patronage, we are willing to repair your gas lawnmower at no cost to you. Consequently, please ship the machine back to us C.O.D. We will repair it and return it to you at our expense.

Please call upon us the next time you need our service. We will see to it that your next experience will be quite satisfactory.

Thanks again for writing.

AMERICAN AIRLINES

633 THIRD AVENUE

NEW YORK, N.Y.

Director Customer Relations

XXXXXXXXXXXXXX
XXXXXXXXXXXXX
XXXXXXXXXXXXX

Dear Mr. Tomlin:

I sincerely regret that we were unable to operate your August 3 flight on time and apologize for the inconvenience it caused you.

Because of our comprehensive maintenance program, we can usually give our customers the dependable service they expect from American Airlines. Once in a while though, there can be unexpected mechanical problems, and I am sorry it happened on your flight.

We will do our best to give you better service as you fly with us in the future—I know we can.

Sincerely yours,

Letter of Apology (General)

• THANKS FOR BUSINESS SUGGESTION

A customer who writes you a letter suggesting an improvement or an addition to your business certainly deserves a reply. That is so whether or not the suggestion is practical.

General Rules

Come right to the point with sincerity and appreciation.
Mention the suggestion for which you are thanking him or her.
Tell the reader what action, if any, is being taken on his or her suggestion.

Alternate Phrases

(a) Thank you very much for your recent letter about Minute Maid orange juice.

I hope you'll forgive me for being so tardy in answering your nice letter suggesting a certified farrier to be featured in our prime time TV show, *Unique People*. I wanted to study the possibility very carefully before making any decision.

Thank you very much for your letter of March 23 in which you suggest a new way of attaching seat belts to our cars.

(b) Your suggestion that we also package grapefruit juice in quart containers has been passed along to those responsible for our new products program. You may be sure it will be given every consideration.

It was brought to my attention, however, that in the past we have featured a horseshoeing person, a farrier if you will, and it didn't work out.

I have forwarded your letter to our research department for further study. As soon as some kind of a conclusion is reached, I will write you to let you know about it.

(c) We sincerely appreciate your kind comments about our products, and thank you for taking the time to write us.

But thanks for thinking of us. And if you have any suggestions in the future, please get in touch with me at *Unique People,* Noel Productions, Hollywood.

Thanks again for your interest and for writing to us.

MICRO ELECTRONICS CORPORATION

WAYCROSS, GEORGIA

Public Relations Department

XXXXXXXXXXXXXX
XXXXXXXXXXXXXX
XXXXXXXXXXXXXX

Dear Ms Klawitt:

Thanks so much for your thoughtful letter suggesting that we replace our plain tabs with laminated tabs in our User's Guide, the instructions manual shipped with our home computer.

After checking into it, we agree with you completely. Laminated tabs do stand up much better under constant usage by our home computer customers than plain tabs.

Consequently, you will be glad to know that as a direct result of your letter, beginning with the next printing, our User's Guide will have laminated tabs to designate the different sections in the manual. And to show our appreciation for your suggestion, we will send you the very first "new look" User's Guide with our compliments.

Thanks again for writing.

Sincerely yours,

Thanks for Business Suggestion

• HOLIDAY GREETINGS

A holiday offers you an ideal opportunity to demonstrate your thoughtfulness to your customers, clients, and distributors. A brief letter expressing a simple but sincere thought is all you need.

General Rules

Give your holiday message warmth and sincerity, but avoid being effusive. Don't make it a sales letter.

Alternate Phrases

(a) Merry Christmas! Happy New Year!

All of us here at the Martin factory wish you and your family a Merry Christmas and the best of everything during the coming year.

Happy holidays! This is the time of year when we think of friends and friends think of us; and that's the way it should be.

(b) Best wishes for a Merry Christmas and a Happy New Year.

May the joy and peace of Christmas be with you now and throughout the New Year.

Wishing you the joys of Christmas and many blessings in the New Year.

I. J. DRESSENBERG

AUSTIN, TEXAS

Christmas time is a welcome break from everyday pressures. . . . .an especially good time to count our blessings. . . . .an appropriate time to say "Thanks sincerely" to our many good customers and friends.

May you have a most enjoyable Christmas and a bountiful, happy New Year.

Cordially,

Holiday Greetings

• ANNIVERSARY OF CUSTOMER'S FIRM OR AN INDIVIDUAL'S SERVICE WITH FIRM

This type of letter is similar to the friendly handshake, where you tell another human being that he or she has done a good job. Everyone appreciates this kind of mail.

General Rules

Avoid the temptation to write an ostentatious or gushy letter.
Try to be specific about why you are complimenting the person.
Make it a personal letter.

Alternate Phrases

(a) You've done the Southern contingent a world of good, Al, in making your way from the plains of Texas to the position of a vice president in the short five years you've trod the Sears path. And here's one member of that group who says, "Congratulations and thanks."

Having observed many times during your ten years with JKL Company that thoughtfulness was one of your charming qualities, I was not surprised to receive your acknowledgement of our 1981 Annual Report. Many thanks for your very nice letter.

It is a great pleasure to congratulate you and offer our best wishes to your organization in its fiftieth year in business.

(b) If I recall correctly, I first met you in Greensboro, and later I had the privilege to be associated with you in a few activities in Memphis. And that takes us about halfway back to your start with the company. During the time I've known you, your representation of Sears has been of the highest order, both at your desk and in the communities you have served.

We, too, are glad that you have been associated with JKL for the past ten years, and we hope you will be with us for a long time. A genuinely warm fellowship and full appreciation will always be yours at this company.

That seems like a long time. But I would be willing to bet that you enjoyed every minute of it, and that your customers were always satisfied with the way you served them.

(c) It's an honor and a pleasure for me to join in the chorus of "Best of luck, Al" that is properly coming your way today.

Best wishes for good health, happiness, and a wonderful future.

Congratulations!

A.E. STALEY MANUFACTURING COMPANY

CORN AND SOYBEAN PRODUCTS

DECATUR, ILLINOIS

Credit Department

XXXXXXXXXXXXXX
XXXXXXXXXXXXX
XXXXXXXXXXXXX

Dear Mr. Lansing:

It is a great satisfaction at the end of the fiscal year to look over those accounts who have given us such wonderful patronage all these many years. Those accounts who regularly, without fail, earn their cash discount by paying our billing promptly. In this group, we are happy and proud to have your company. A greatly appreciated group whom, you can rest assured, we will never take for granted.

I understand that you are in your fiftieth year of business. Coincidentally, we are also celebrating our golden anniversary this year. In the glow of our mutually rich experience, may we, in all sincerity, step forward and extend our hand and say "Congratulations!" May there be many more golden years.

Sincerely,

Credit Manager
xx/xx

**Anniversary of Customer's Firm or
an Individual's Service with Firm**

• ANNIVERSARY OF START OF BUSINESS WITH CUSTOMER

Sending this type of letter is a thoughtful gesture, one the customer/client will certainly appreciate. Besides, it's a good customer relations letter without being a sales letter.

General Rules

Mention the number of years the customer/client has been with you.
Express your appreciation of his or her patronage and/or trust in you.
Tell of your anticipation of many more years of this mutually satisfactory relationship.

Alternate Phrases

(a) It is a distinct pleasure to note that it is now ten years since you opened an account with us. The pleasant relationship with customers of long standing is one of the nice things about being in business.

We are happy to observe that your account has now been with us for fifteen years. The client-stockbroker relationship is unique, and we are proud to have your trust.

Today is the "Golden Anniversary" of the ABC Company's account with us, for it was opened just fifty years ago.

(b) I sincerely hope that your dealings with us have been satisfactory, and I assure you we will make every effort to maintain and improve our services so that we may serve you even better in the future.

Business relationships of that length cannot be mere coincidences. They reflect mutual benefit and helpfulness. And you can be certain that we will do our best to continue to merit your confidence for the next fifteen years.

All of us here at the XYZ Company join me in extending to you and your staff our heartiest thanks. We regard it as an honor of the highest order to have merited your patronage for so long a period.

(c) Best wishes to you.

Permit us to wish you and your company continued success and progress in the years to come.

Fifty years have brought vast changes in banking. What has not changed, however, is the spirit of mutual helpfulness and good will which has always marked our relations with you. Again, best wishes to you always.

MANUFACTURERS HANOVER TRUST COMPANY

330 PARK AVENUE, N.Y., N.Y.

XXXXXXXXXXXXXXX
XXXXXXXXXXXXXX
XXXXXXXXXXXXXX

Dear Mr. Brown:

More than a generation ago . . . . thirty-five years ago to be exact . . . . the ABC Company first favored us with an account. We wish to mark this important anniversary by telling you how much this long-standing relationship has meant to us.

Manufacturers Hanover Trust Company was then a small bank and the growth we have enjoyed since that time has been due in large measure to the confidence and loyalty of our many friends.

We are happy to include you among these friends, and hope that as the years go by we can continue to make our services even broader and more useful to you and your organization.

Sincerely,

Anniversary of Start of Business with Customer

• THANK YOU LETTER FOR MAKING SPECIAL EFFORT

A letter of thanks to someone who has made a special effort in your behalf is an excellent way to promote customer relations. But don't forget the people in your own company; they like a pat on the back, too.

General Rules

Thank the person(s), and recognize that a specific effort was made.
If feasible, tell how it helped you.

Alternate Phrases

(a) Last week when a serious mechanical problem in our computer mainframe brought down all the systems we called upon Mr. Holroyd, your systems engineer, at his home. And even though it was in the middle of the night, he came immediately to our computer center. After working on it for five hours, Mr. Holroyd solved the problem, and by 6 a.m. the systems were up and running.

I want to thank you for your recent donation to the Mercy Hospital Blood Bank.

After our recent fire which all but paralyzed production in our main plant and resulted in delayed delivery for almost six weeks, you displayed every consideration we could ask for.

(b) Cooperation such as this at inconvenient hours means a great deal, and we wish to extend our sincere thanks to you and particularly to Mr. Holroyd for his assistance.

We take great pride in your reaction to urgent community need, and I am certain that you will be most pleased to learn that your contribution saved a life.

This is just a brief note to express our very great appreciation to you for bearing with us during this difficult period. We can only hope that we have not inconvenienced you too much.

(c) Thanks again for your cooperation, we will remember it.

You deserve a hearty handshake for a job well done and a sincere thank you.

As you know, we are once again operating at full efficiency and hope to catch up with our deliveries within the next few days. Your account will be the first to be serviced. Once again, thanks ever so much.

JOHN WANAMAKER
PHILADELPHIA, INC.

To the Store Family:

My heartiest thanks to each and every one of you for making such a fine effort to be on the job during the brutal three weeks of the transportation strike.

Such loyalty and devotion on the part of our Store Family have been two of the chief reasons for our success over the years.

With the strike now over and with a most impressive sale coming up, starting this Friday, I would hope that all of us could regain the momentum we lost and have the best Spring in our history.

Again, thank you.

President

Thank You Letter for Making Special Effort

• THANKS FOR FAVOR

At one time or another you probably had to ask business associates or friends for special favors. Whatever other gesture of appreciation you might make, a letter is always appropriate and always welcome.

General Rules

Specify the favor, and how it helped you.
Be sincere in giving your thanks.
Offer to reciprocate in the future.

Alternate Phrases

(a) It was wonderful of you to spend the time you did collecting so much useful material for me. Just as soon as I finish my article, I will send it to you for your comments.

Thank you so much for the favor you did for me. No one could have been more generous than you in your support of me before the board.

I want to thank you for doing me the personal favor of talking with Nelson Kranford.

(b) I realize that gathering all this information, not only from your personal files, but from so many of your friends and acquaintances, required a considerable amount of time, time you no doubt could have used to your own advantage.

It is easy to understand why you have gained the reputation of a man who doesn't mind sticking his neck out to help a person whose back is up against the wall. I envy your reputation as well as your courage.

Nelson told me about the many helpful suggestions you gave him. He thinks he now has a clearer picture of the situation, and can make an intelligent decision.

(c) Thanks again for your help. If I can reciprocate at any time in the future, be sure to call upon me.

Again, many thanks for your support.

It was wonderful of you to give him so much of your valuable time, and to make his visit with you so helpful. We both appreciate it very much, and look forward to reciprocating your kindness.

A.G. ROBERTS CO.

700 CRESTVIEW AVENUE

DENNIS, ILLINOIS

XXXXXXXXXXXXXX
XXXXXXXXXXXXXX
XXXXXXXXXXXXXX

Dear Ms Christian:

I want to thank you and tell you how much I appreciate all the favors you have done for me during my recent business crisis. It would not have been possible for anyone to be more kind than you were.

I can readily understand how you, personally, as well as your company, have earned the respect and admiration of everyone in the field. You certainly deserve your wonderful reputation.

If there's ever an occasion when I can return your kindness, please let me know. It would be a distinct pleasure for me to be able to reciprocate.

Sincerely yours,

Thanks for Favor

5

Tasteful Letters for Contracting and Dealing with Products and/or Services

Before supplies are purchased, before equipment is leased or purchased, or before services are contracted for, a variety of precise letters have to be written. These letters are very important because you have to be explicit, accurate, and thorough both in asking for information and in defining the specifications for a bid or an order. Inaccuracy or incompleteness can be costly to all concerned. This is especially true when asking for a bid from several vendors. For example, your letter (if no formal Request for Proposal is prepared) must clearly stipulate the responsibilities of both your company (the customer/user) and the vendor. This is only one of the many critical issues that your letter must deal with in contracting for product(s) and/or services.

In many cases, your reason for writing may be to ask for an improved delivery date or some other special consideration because of an unforeseen development. Here, in addition to being specific about what you want done and why it is important, you need to be persuasive.

Another letter you may have to write is one insisting on better handling of your orders, or complaining about the services, or the way an order was shipped.

This chapter will help you cope with these types of letter-writing problems, and do it easily and quickly. Notice that even large corporations' letters to delinquent vendors are tactful. Most modern businessmen believe that brute force is too costly in the long run. It doesn't pay to jeopardize future relations with others in the business community by being crude and/or rude.

The samples you will find in this chapter are worded to get positive results without alienating a vendor who just may be able to help you out in some future emergency.

125

• REQUESTING INFORMATION FROM VENDOR

Your letter to a vendor asking for information about products or services should be as specific as you can make it, especially if you are writing to a firm that has not dealt with you before.

General Rules

State clearly and completely the information you want.
Don't suggest the possibility of an order if none exists.

Alternate Phrases

(a) How soon can you deliver 3,000 order pads of the same size and quality as the enclosed sample?

We are designing several piping systems that will require the extensive use of stainless steel pipes, fittings, and valves. Specifications call for Type 316 throughout, in a wide range of sizes, with pressures up to 3,000 PSI.

We are preparing next season's catalog and would like to include stained glass art. Would you send us a list of the items you have available?

(b) In your reply please also state if you have window envelopes for this size paper.

Could you send us a catalog of any material you can supply for such service? It will not be necessary for a sales representative to call at this time.

We are especially interested in art work from local stained glass artists.

(c) We need these pads as soon as we can get them, so please give this request your prompt attention.

The information we ask for will be most helpful to us.

Thank you for your cooperation.

TACOMA COMPANY INC.

MANUFACTURER OF HEATING AND AIR CONDITIONING PRODUCTS

BOULDERS, ILLINOIS

Wang Laboratories, Inc.
One Industrial Ave.
Lowell, Massachusetts 01851

Gentlemen:

Since we are thinking of replacing our electronic typewriters with a word processing computer system in the near future, we would be interested in getting detailed information about your "Wangwriter."

Specifically, we want to know its capabilities, its price, its maintenance cost, and its modularity. Also, please include information about documentation that accompanies the Wangwriter and how much training you provide the clerical staff for the system.

We shall await an early reply.

Yours truly,

Purchasing Director
XX/xx

Requesting Information from Vendor

• ASKING FOR BIDS

Most large and even medium size companies normally send out a detailed Request for Proposals (RFP) or a Request for Quotation (RFQ) with a cover letter whenever they plan to buy merchandise, buy or rent equipment, and/or contract for services. If the product is not significant enough to warrant writing even a simple, informal RFP, state your requirements in a letter. Written requests for bids prevent any misunderstanding and discussions at a later date. If bids have to be made by telephone, get confirmation in writing as soon as possible.

General Rules

State clearly and completely what information you're looking for.

Give all the information necessary to the vendor so that he or she can respond completely to your formal or informal RFP or RFQ or letter.

Specify when you need the product and/or service.

Alternate Phrases

(a) Attached is Drawing No. 40322, showing a walkway from the precipitator to the stack. Please quote in triplicate the cost of furnishing this walkway, ready for erection, but not erected, including one coat of shop paint.

Please send us your quotation on the items listed on the attached pages at your earliest convenience.

We are pleased to invite you to submit a proposal for landscaping services around the Corporate Headquarters building.

(b) If you have any questions concerning this project, please contact Mr. L. Crinic, Plant Engineer.

The listed items are needed to be sent to four distribution points in the South and the Midwest.

The Company currently has a contract with a firm that provides landscaping services which will expire next month.

(c) Quotations are to be addressed to Mr. Joseph G. Smith, Vice President, Purchases and Raw Materials.

Please include in your quotation packaging as well as shipping costs.

It is anticipated that a contractor will be selected not later than September 10, 198_ to provide us complete landscaping services for the next three years. Consequently, all the proposals will have to be on Mr. Smith's desk no later than noon, September 1, 198_.

AMERICAN STEEL COMPANY

ALLENTOWN, PENNSYLVANIA

TO: Prospective Contractors

FROM: Department of Purchase and Contract
Contractual Services Section

SUBJECT: Request for Proposals (RFP) Dated
April 8, 198_
For an Employee Health Insurance
Program

PURPOSE: American Steel Company desires to contract with an independent firm to process and pay claims for the Company's all-inclusive Employee Health Insurance Program. The proposed system to process, validate, verify, and pay the claims is expected to be a highly efficient and cost-beneficial computer system.

TIME: The sealed cost and technical proposals under separate cover and subject to conditions stated in the attached RFP will be received until 2:00 p.m., May 28, 198_ for furnishing services as described herein.

NOTE: Indicate the firm's name and address, and the words "Cost Proposal" or "Technical Proposal" on the front of each sealed envelope, along with the date for receipt of proposals.

Asking for Bids/Request for Proposals

• PLACING THE ORDER/AWARDING THE CONTRACT

The primary rule in placing an order or awarding a contract is to be thorough. The order should be definitive as to what products you want, date of expected delivery, and so on. The contract and the cover letter that accompanies the contract should be precise and complete.

General Rules

Give full details of the order or the service. Leave no chance for misunderstanding.

If the delivery date or starting date of service is especially important, emphasize it in the order or the service contract.

Alternate Phrases

(a) We are pleased to enclose our Purchase Order, No. 10429 for the material as quoted in your estimate of March 7.

Please send us the items exactly as listed in your letter of July 1.

We are once again pleased to award you our contract for providing twenty-four-hour security guards for our R&D plant in Raleigh, N.C. The price stated in this two-year contract shall constitute complete consideration for the services provided by the Contractor, except as otherwise specifically stated in the attached contract.

(b) Will you please make every effort to ship this material in the required time? Our customer has given us a firm deadline.

We must receive these items by Nov. 26, so that we can fulfill our commitments.

Attached please find our contract in triplicate. After signing the contract, please return two copies to us. The third copy is for your files.

(c) Your cooperation will be appreciated.

Thank you for the promptness with which you have handled this transaction, and trust that our order will be filled just as promptly.

The last two years we have been quite pleased with the services you provided, and we trust that we will be just as satisfied with your next two years' security services.

FLORIDA FEDERAL SAVINGS AND LOAN ASSOCIATION

JACKSONVILLE, FLORIDA

XXXXXXXXXXXXXX
XXXXXXXXXXXXXX
XXXXXXXXXXXXXX

Gentlemen:

We are pleased to inform you that we have decided to award you the landscaping project, based on your proposal of January 16, 198__.

We would appreciate your starting immediately the landscaping around our new Corporate Headquarters building at 44 Landau Avenue, Jacksonville, FL, because as we stated in our RFP, the work must be completed not later than February 12, 198__. This is crucial, since the opening of our new building is scheduled for February 15.

Please sign the attached two copies of the contract, and return the original to us as soon as possible.

Sincerely,

Placing an Order/Awarding a Contract

• REJECTING THE BID

Rejecting bids is a necessary part of business. In many cases, however, a vendor who loses out is left guessing as to the reason. A letter in this situation is a courtesy that is appreciated.

General Rules

Thank the bidder for the time and effort he or she put into preparing a proposal or a quotation.

Tell the vendor why his or her bid has been rejected.

Keep the door open for future transactions.

Alternate Phrases

(a) The quality of your quotation of May 10 reflected the time and effort you must have expended.

We appreciate your efforts in preparing the proposal you submitted to us.

Thank you for the comprehensive, well-written bid you submitted to us for _____.

(b) We are unable to grant you this contract because we need the merchandise sooner than you can supply it.

We are sorry that the quantities we need are more than your company is equipped to handle.

We regret that we are unable to give you a contract for this project, because the specifications in your bid do not meet our requirements as stated in our RFP.

(c) We will continue to invite you to submit quotations, and hope that the next time we will be able to accept yours.

The excellent reputation of your company makes it highly probable that the next contract will go to you.

We have had transactions in the past, and I hope we will have many more in the future.

K.B. DOLL CORPORATION

346 CARROLL STREET

BROOKLYN, N.Y.

Purchasing Department

XXXXXXXXXXXXXX
XXXXXXXXXXXXXX
XXXXXXXXXXXXXX

Dear _____:

    Thank you for the time and effort you spent in preparing your proposal of January 16.

    We regret to inform you that we are giving this contract to another vendor because of price considerations.

    Be assured that you will be included in any future invitations to bid.

                           Sincerely,

Rejecting the Bid

• COMPLIMENTING THE VENDOR

Complimenting a vendor for doing a job with which you are particularly pleased gives him or her the incentive to repeat the same performance with your next contract or order. This is an easy and pleasant letter to write, and it can bring many dividends of goodwill to your business.

General Rules

Be sincere when complimenting the vendor.

Be specific as to the incident or service about which you are complimenting the vendor.

Make it a personal letter.

Alternate Phrases

(a) For the past month we have had several demanding situations that required fast action from you.

Last week we found ourselves in a very difficult situation. We turned to you for help, and you certainly obliged us in a most satisfactory manner.

When a vendor puts all his resources at the command of a customer, he creates a bond between them.

(b) We would like to take time out to thank you and your staff for the excellent service you provided us.

We want to thank you for your unstinting cooperation that helped us out in a trying moment.

Thanks for your generous cooperation.

(c) Please convey our particular thanks to your engineering department for a commendable job.

We look forward to a continued mutually favorable relationship.

In the future, when we want a good job done, we will come to you again.

AMERICAN BOSCH ARMA CORPORATION

GARDEN CITY,

NEW YORK

XXXXXXXXXXXXXXX
XXXXXXXXXXXXXX
XXXXXXXXXXXXXX

Dear Mr. Swift:

Over the years we have enjoyed a most satisfactory relationship with your company to our mutual benefit.

Every once in a while, however, your ingenious and inventive staff does something outstanding that is above the normal vendor-customer relationship. Such was the case recently, when your organization produced an unsolicited prototype data-base management system (DBMS) package for our microcomputer system.

On behalf of the Management, Procurement, and Engineering personnel, please accept our sincere appreciation for anticipating our needs.

Sincerely yours,

Complimenting the Vendor

• COMPLAINT TO VENDOR

If there are any problems with the service, merchandise, delivery or shipping, or goods damaged in transit, you should immediately write a letter to the vendor. This way the problem can be corrected before it becomes unmanageable. Besides, how will the vendor know that there's a problem if you don't communicate it to him or her?

General Rules

Be specific about what your complaint is and what you want done.

Be fair in describing the problem. Don't make the proverbial mountain out of a mole-hill. Give specific suggestions for correcting the problem, if you can.

Alternate Phrases

(a) A company's good reputation is its most important asset. We prize ours as I'm sure you do yours. That's why I want to call your attention to defective materials in your last shipment.

I am sure you will agree that we have had a good business relationship for many years. It is for that reason that your sudden raising of the price of _____ came as a shock to us.

We all try to do the best job we can for our customers. That's how we stay in business; that's how we grow. When the rare occasion occurs that we goof, we sure want to hear about it. I know you feel the same way. That's why I want to talk to you about the service you have been providing us with the last two weeks.

(b, c) The defects that I am talking about are _____. I am attaching a copy of our engineer's report so you can see exactly what has to be corrected.

As far as we know, nothing has happened in the industry to warrant an increase in price. If you felt justified in this action, why didn't you discuss it with us instead of acting unilaterally?

As you know, our contract calls for _____. The satisfactory fulfillment of this agreement is essential to the operation of our business.

(d) I'm sure that this letter is all that's needed to get you to correct the defects. Thank you for your cooperation.

I hope that you will reconsider your action. Please call me if you want a further clarification of our position.

Thank you for your cooperation.

AMERICAN BOSCH ARMA CORPORATION

GARDEN CITY,

NEW YORK

XXXXXXXXXXXXXX
XXXXXXXXXXXXXX
XXXXXXXXXXXXXX

Gentlemen:

Your attention is called to a serious delivery problem concerning our Purchase Order No. H8016 so that you can initiate immediate correction.

We have repeatedly communicated with your personnel to revert the schedule to our required date of May 8, 198_ without success. The delay in delivery of your components seriously compromises final delivery of instruments against a prime Air Force weapons contract. The New York Air Force Contract Management District is being alerted to this delay by a copy of this letter.

We therefore urge you to take all necessary steps to assure the Air Force and ourselves that delivery will be made as contractually required.

Please assure us by return mail that you are giving this problem your personal and urgent attention.

Yours truly,

Complaint to Vendor

• CANCELING THE ORDER OR CONTRACT

Sometimes, due to circumstances you will have to cancel an order or a contract. A letter explaining your position will usually do the job, although complicated problems will have to be worked out by your legal department.

General Rules

Make it clear that you are canceling the order or contract.
Give a reason for the cancelation.
Be courteous. You may want to do business with the company in the future.

Alternate Phrases

(a) Please cancel our order number RL4421.

We regret that circumstances force us to cancel our order of June 9.

Confirming our telephone conversation of yesterday, we are canceling our data processing service contract with you as of September 1, 198_.

(b) The deadline for delivery of this material is long past and we can no longer wait for it.

The order we had for water distillation units has been canceled, so we no longer need your materials.

As we told you, we have installed a computer system at our office, and our staff is taking care of all our data processing needs.

(c) We regret the necessity for this cancelation but are sure that, as a business person yourself, you understand.

You have no doubt found yourself in a similar position and were as unhappy about that cancelation as we are about this one. We hope that our next transaction will be more satisfactory.

We have been satisfied with the services you provided, but we believe that in-house data processing will prove to be more economical.

PREMIER ELECTRONICS COMPANY

455 GAINSBORO AVENUE
TALUSA, SOUTH CAROLINA

XXXXXXXXXXXXXX
XXXXXXXXXXXXXX
XXXXXXXXXXXXXX

Dear Ms _____:

Since you are still not able to send us the material listed in our Purchase Order #24689, we are forced to cancel our order. As you know, we need these items to complete our order to our Australian account.

The customer in Sydney informed us that they can no longer wait for this material. Consequently, the shipment is being sent without your merchandise.

We are sorry this cancelation is necessary. But we are sure you realize that we have no other choice.

Yours truly,

Canceling the Order or Contract

• DECLINING TO DO BUSINESS

A letter explaining why you aren't buying a company's product or service is a courtesy that is often overlooked. These samples will make it simple to get such letters written, and keep lines open to potential vendors.

General Rules

Thank the vendor for the offer of merchandise or service.
Explain why you decline to buy at this time.
Hold out the possibility of future business transactions.

Alternate Phrases

(a) Thank you for submitting your 19–– catalog of products to us. We appreciate your thoughtfulness.

Thank you for bringing your samples down to my office, and for telling me about the benefits your products could be to our company.

Thank you for the interesting and informative talk you gave at my office last week.

(b) It is not common knowledge yet, but we are eliminating two of our lines—the "bracket" line included. While this action will not completely eliminate our need for your products, it cuts down the amount we use. Therefore, for the time being, we have a sufficient supply of materials on hand.

We know that yours is a first-rate company manufacturing a first-rate product, and we would ordinarily be happy to deal with you. But we have been doing business with another vendor for many years, and are quite satisfied with their products and service. We are not, therefore, planning any change in the near future.

As you know, business has not been up to expectations so far this year. Therefore, for the time being, we will not be needing any outside data processing service bureau.

(c) Thanks again for writing, and please keep our name on your active mailing list.

I can assure you that should we decide to change vendors at any time in the future, your company will be carefully considered.

As soon as we are ready to contract outside data processing services, however, you can be sure that we will contact you.

GEORGIA-PACIFIC CORPORATION

EQUITABLE BUILDING

PORTLAND, OREGON

XXXXXXXXXXXXXXX
XXXXXXXXXXXXXX
XXXXXXXXXXXXXX

Dear Mr._____ :

Thank you for bringing your Canadian interests to our attention. We buy a good deal of veneer in Canada now, and also a few logs from time to time. Our use of logs is not extensive and probably will decrease rather than increase, due to recent connections made for the purchases of veneer on a contractual arrangement.

No one, of course, knows just how fast our needs will develop, or how our current supplier's operations will work out. Consequently, it would be our pleasure to talk with you from time to time about the products you have available. However, at present we would be in no position to make any definite commitments.

Sincerely,

Declining to Do Business

6

Productive Letters That Deal with Financial Matters

L etters written to bankers, financial institutions, insurance companies, government agencies, overseas contacts, and financial officers primarily deal with financial matters. Whether they discuss a special banking group plan proposed by a bank, checks returned because of insufficient funds, credit policy, or request for information about a possible investment or an overseas customer/vendor, these letters minimize misunderstanding as well as promote good relationships.

The samples in this chapter cover most of the types of letters you will need when writing a letter of financial concern. All you need to do is modify names and insert the appropriate data.

• LETTER TO BANKERS

Your letter to a banker is often one of request, with emphasis on information. But equally often, your letter is one of appreciation. In either case, clarity, completeness, and graciousness are the ingredients of any effective letter to a banker.

General Rules

Avoid formal language. It's obsolete, Use simple, direct language.
Be businesslike and get to the point quickly.
Be sure that you express clearly what information you're seeking.

Alternate Phrases

(a) This is to confirm our telephone conversation about stopping the payment of one of our checks.

The overseas company named above gave your bank as a reference. Consequently, we would appreciate any information you can give us about this company, which may become an important customer.

For many years now we have been receiving our monthly statement from you at the end of each month. For the past three months we didn't get our statement until the 12th of the following month.

(b) The check number is _____, date _____, made out to _____, in the amount of _____.

We particularly would like to know this company's manner of handling accounts payable in this country, and your impression of the company's management.

I'm sure you realize that receiving the statement this late makes our accounting needlessly difficult. Your cooperation will be very much appreciated in ensuring that this month's statement and subsequent ones are sent to us on time.

(c) If there is any further information you need, please let me know.

Thank you for any information you can give us. We assure you your comments will be held in strict confidence.

Thank you for your immediate attention to this matter.

LUKENS STEEL COMPANY

COATESVILLE, PENNSYLVANIA

XXXXXXXXXXXXXX
XXXXXXXXXXXXXX
XXXXXXXXXXXXXX

Gentlemen:

Your proposal to provide our 2,500 employees your Special Banking Group Program is gratefully accepted by management. We relayed your offer to the Employees Union, and its consensus agreed with us that it is a money-saving service for the union members.

Though the Employees Union is writing you an acceptance letter, I wanted to write to you personally to tell you how much I appreciate your offer of providing free checking accounts with no minimum balance required, free travelers checks, and free safety deposit boxes to our employees.

Your bank has been servicing the Lukens Steel Company most satisfactorily for almost a decade. Now, all our employees will have a chance to enjoy your excellent services also.

Sincerely,

John Q. Donald
President
JQD:fs

Letter to Bankers

• LETTER TO FINANCIAL INSTITUTIONS

The letter you write to financial institutions can be a request for information, or a proposal (estimate) for a project you want them to do for you. It can also be a letter of thanks.

General Rules

Be specific and concise.
Use informal and clear language.
Be sincere when complimenting the addressee.

Alternate Phrases

(a) We understand that you have compiled and presented in a report the latest financial data on Fortune 500 U.S. corporations. Being one of those corporations, we would like to receive that particular report.

We appreciate your prompt response to our request to send us your literature on the different types of pension plans and IRAs.

As financial advisors to our firm, we would like to have one of your senior analysts speak at our next corporate meeting on October 12.

(b) Quite frankly, we are rather surprised that you have not included us in your mailing list for the report above. Of course, oversights do occur even in the best run firms.

Thanks to you, our employees now can choose between the Company Pension Plan, private pension plans and IRA. They appreciate having all the pros and cons presented to them objectively and in depth as in your brochures.

All our executives are interested in learning about Certificates of Deposit, T-Bills and Money Market Certificates, and the latest data on interest rates.

(c) Your immediate attention to this matter will be appreciated.

Again, thank you.

Please let us know which of your senior staff will be able to speak at the meeting. We are looking forward to his or her presentation.

MICRO ELECTRONICS CORPORATION

WAYCROSS, GEORGIA

XXXXXXXXXXXXXX
XXXXXXXXXXXXXX
XXXXXXXXXXXXXX

Dear _____:

Because we have used your investment counseling services before and were satisfied, once again we are seeking your expert advice.

As you know, the Company has been investing in several real estate sites, but management feels that perhaps we should diversify by investing in certain low-priced stocks.

What we want from you is an evaluation and prognosis on how some attractive low-priced stocks such as PROX, MED, or BURR on the American Exchange might do. Specifically, we want to know, which of these or other stocks—in your opinion—will be the "high fliers" of tomorrow?

Before your financial analysts start working on our assignment, however, please give us a written estimate as to the cost and time-frame of this project.

Sincerely,

Letter to Financial Institutions

• LETTER TO CREDIT BUREAUS

The letter you send to credit bureaus is more often than not a request for information about a potential customer or vendor. It also can be a letter demanding to see your own company's credit history because it has come to your attention that the credit bureau erred.

General Rules

Be clear and definitive about the information you need.
Be courteous, even when you're sure the credit bureau has made a mistake.

Alternate Phrases

(a) Please send us any information you have about XYZ Company, Edison, N.J. We are thinking of buying electronics testing equipment from them, however, we don't know very much about them.

It has come to our attention that, according to a report you have sent to one of our suppliers, we have not paid a certain overdue account.

(b) It's very important to us that our vendors are solid, established companies with good credit rating. We don't want to deal with any vendor who may not be around six months from now.

That is an error. The creditor in question sent us damaged merchandise on June 29, 198_. It was returned to the vendor promptly on June 30, 198_, canceling the order at the same time. Attached please find a xerox copy of the cancelation.

(c) I'm sure you can understand our concern and will send us the requested information at your earliest convenience. Thank you.

Please correct the error immediately and send us a copy of our updated credit report for our approval.

A. G. ROBERTS COMPANY

700 CRESTVIEW AVENUE

DENNIS, ILLINOIS

XXXXXXXXXXXXXX
XXXXXXXXXXXXX
XXXXXXXXXXXXXX

Dear _____:

Because we anticipate a rather large order from Simco, Inc., of San Diego, California, we would appreciate getting from you a "credit profile" of this company.

We understand that as a credit bureau you don't make any recommendations or comments about any firm. However, the credit history of the company above will be sufficient for us to make a determination as to whether we should extend credit to them or not.

Thank you for your cooperation.

Yours truly,

Letter to Credit Bureaus

• LETTER TO CREDITORS

The letter you write to creditors usually is compact and specific. The samples in this section will simplify your task of writing such difficult letters, yet keep the communication lines open.

General Rules

Make the letter simple and straightforward.
Be courteous. You may need this creditor in the future.
If in arrears with payment, explain the circumstances.

Alternate Phrases

(a)   We are very sorry that we will be unable to meet the interest payment due this month.

     We are sorry to let you know that payment for the merchandise you shipped us a month ago will be late.

     We were quite disturbed when the bank notified us that our check #20957 in the amount of $8540.00, was returned to you, marked "insufficient funds."

(b)   We are in this embarrassing situation on account of a newly announced government regulation that is delaying us from starting to sell our completed one-family houses on schedule. You can imagine what this slippage is costing us.

     Perhaps you have heard that one of our warehouses was destroyed in a fire. Luckily, the merchandise you shipped to us was in another warehouse, nevertheless, the loss we have suffered affected our whole operation.

     Because our account is in excellent shape, we immediately contacted the bank. Some time later, one of the bank's vice presidents, Mr. Ederson, called back and apologized for the mistake.

(c)   However, now that our houses are at long last on the market, you can expect our regular payment next month together with this month's payment, plus the late interest charges.

     Please be assured that we will pay you as soon as possible. In the meantime, your understanding and patience will be greatly appreciated.

     Mr. Ederson promised us to send a letter to you apologizing for the inconvenience the bank's mistake may have caused you. So please redeposit our check. Be assured that it will be honored.

PLACER COUNTY
DISTRICT ATTORNEY

COURTHOUSE

AUBURN, CALIFORNIA

March 25, 198_

Brown-Foreman Company, Inc.
Owings Mills, California

Re: Estate of_____, deceased.
    Placer County Probate No._____.

Gentlemen:

Mr._____ died in Placer County on January 22, 198_.

His estate consists of the following:

_____

_____

If there should be any amount due you, the estate will be happy to make payment upon your submission of a creditor's claim.

If there are any amounts due or payable, they should be paid to me as the executor of the will of Mr._____, deceased. **Letters Testamentary** will be furnished to you upon notice of funds to be payable to the estate.

Yours very truly,

Daniel J. Higgins
District Attorney and
Public Administrator

*Through the courtesy of Mr. Dan Higgins, Placer County District Attorney,
Auburn, California*

Letter to Creditors

• LETTER TO DEBTORS

The primary objective of the letter you write to debtors is to get the money that is due to you. It should be simple, direct, and courteous. You may want to do business with a particular debtor in the future. That is, if he or she honors the debt, or in the case of a bad check, makes good the amount.

General Rules

Be concise and to the point.
State the amount and the date when payment was due.
Be specific. Ask the exact date when you can expect the payment in full.

Alternate Phrases

(a) The "interest-alone" payment on your loan was due on the 15th of this month. Today is the 27th, and we still have not received your payment.

Payment on your revolving charge account was due two weeks ago.

The rental on your photography store is overdue. According to the contract you signed on October 3, 198_, your monthly payment must reach us by the 15th of each month.

(b) If you are unable to make this month's payment, we would appreciate your letting us know the circumstances and also when we may expect your payment.

Could it have been an oversight on your part not to send us the payment? If that is the case, please send us your check by return mail.

Perhaps you are not aware of this payment due, or perhaps you are experiencing temporary financial difficulties. In either case, please get in touch with us immediately.

(c) Please call us at your earliest convenience.

Thank you for your cooperation.

We are looking forward to hearing from you.

PLACER COUNTY
DISTRICT ATTORNEY

COURTHOUSE

AUBURN, CALIFORNIA

XXXXXXXXXXXXXXX
XXXXXXXXXXXXXX
XXXXXXXXXXXXXX

RE: Your Check No. 2055 for $1400.00
     Payable to Robert Franken, Jeweler
     Dated: March 18, 198__.

Dear Miss Robins:

Mr. Franken came to my office and told me that the above check has been returned from Chase National Bank in New York, N.Y. with the notation "Refer to Maker."

In matters such as this, we first contact the maker of the check to learn of the circumstances from that person's point of view.

Please call this office at your earliest convenience for an appointment to discuss the matter.

Yours very truly,

Daniel J. Higgins
District Attorney

Letter to Debtors

7

Successful
Marketing and Sales
Department Letters

Most letters written in the course of business are important to the writer as well as the reader. Obviously, however, none are more vital to business than the marketing and sales letters.

Many types of business letters don't produce immediate and/or discernible results. This is generally not the case with marketing and sales letters; either they bring in the order or contract, or at least an inquiry, or they don't. Consequently, the marketing and sales letters offer a challenge to the letter writer. The letters that he or she writes are either clearly effective or just as clearly ineffective.

Marketing and sales letters stand out above all others as bread-and-butter letters. When you can handle them successfully, you earn a definite reward, not only in terms of money but also in terms of personal satisfaction.

This chapter has been designed as a guide to help you write marketing and sales letters that work. In each case, the sample letters were drafted by successful writers on behalf of the country's leading corporations.

• ANSWERING AN INFORMATION REQUEST

The letter answering an inquiry or a request is an important step in getting an order. Write it carefully; it can be one of your best sales tools.

General Rules

Thank the writer for the inquiry.

Be gracious and to the point. Enclose relevant literature, but don't overwhelm the recipient with a lot of illustrative material.

Offer any other assistance you can.

Alternate Phrases

(a) We appreciate your interest in the Foster-Bateman Company, and are sending you—under separate cover—a copy of our current annual report. We are also forwarding an issue of "Spotlight," our quarterly publication to shareholders, to bring you up to date on the Foster-Bateman operations.

Your continued interest in the home improvement field is gratifying. We are, of course, well aware of your accomplishments in this area, and will pass on to you whatever helpful suggestions we can.

Thank you for your inquiry about the Tru-Built Recreation Vehicles. Descriptive literature covering the particular type of RV you are interested in is enclosed.

(b) To give you a total picture of the company, we are enclosing a descriptive brochure about our manufacturing plants, a copy of our latest sales and earnings release, and a brief company history.

Some of our people are closer to this particular area than I am. Consequently, I am asking Mr. Stevens to carefully study your request, and get in touch with you directly as soon as he can.

There is a sales and service outlet located near you. I have contacted Mr. McCloud, the manager, and he will be most pleased to give you full details concerning specifications, price, and delivery.

(c) Please feel free to call upon us for information or assistance at any time.

It was good of you to write, and I hope Mr. Stevens will be of help to you.

Mr. McCloud will get in touch with you soon, but if in the meantime I can be of any assistance, be sure to let me know.

TEXAS INSTRUMENTS

INCORPORATED

DALLAS, TX

Semiconductor Division

XXXXXXXXXXXXXX
XXXXXXXXXXXXX
XXXXXXXXXXXXX

Dear _____:

Thank you for your interest in Texas Instruments products. It's our pleasure to enclose the information you requested.

Over the past decade, TI has developed and produced literally hundreds of millions of semiconductor devices for the computer industry. We sincerely hope that our broad experience, technological know-how and extensive mechanized production facilities can be of service to you, both now and in the years ahead.

Please let me know if I can be of further assistance. Or, contact your TI sales engineer; he's as near as your telephone.

Sincerely,

Answering an Information Request

• INFORMATION REQUEST REFUSED

The letter of refusal will, of course, disappoint the addressee. You can overcome or at least reduce any possible resultant bad effects by making the letter sincere and friendly.

General Rules

Use tact.
Explain clearly and concisely the reason for your refusal.
Offer to help in the future, if possible.
Express appreciation for the individual's interest in your company.

Alternate Phrases

(a) Thank you for your letter of March 7 in which you ask for information about our computer network security system.

Your letter of October 1 has just been brought to my attention.

Thank you for your letter of May 28. We appreciate that you addressed your inquiry to us.

(b) We would be pleased to send you the information if it were available for public distribution. Unfortunately, it is not.

We would be happy to furnish you with information, if we only knew the type of data you require.

We are sorry, but we cannot comply with your request because our company no longer manufactures photographic equipment.

(c) If the information you want is made available to the public in the near future, we would be pleased to send it to you.

If you can be more specific in your request, we will be pleased to send you the needed data.

We might suggest that this information may be obtained from the National Bureau of Standards, U.S. Government Printing Office.

(d) Thank you for thinking of us. Please write us again if you think we can be of assistance.

Please write us again. We may be able to help you the next time.

While we were unable to be of assistance this time, if you need any information about our main product, microcomputers, please don't hesitate to write us.

PARKER PUBLISHING COMPANY, INC.

VILLAGE SQUARE BUILDING

WEST NYACK, NEW YORK

XXXXXXXXXXXXXX
XXXXXXXXXXXXXX
XXXXXXXXXXXXXX

Dear _____:

Thank you for your letter of April 14, and for your kind comments about our company.

We would be happy to send you a copy of the pamphlet you want if the supply had not been completely exhausted by an unexpectedly heavy demand.

There is a definite possibility, however, that we may reprint the pamphlet next month. If we do, I will see to it that a copy is sent to you immediately.

If we can be of service to you in any other way, please let us know.

Sincerely yours,

Information Request Refused

• FOLLOW-UP SALES OR MARKETING LETTER

A sincere letter thanking the potential customer for attending a sales seminar, coming to your company's booth at an exhibition, or asking for your literature, is essential for reinforcing the prospective customer's interest in your product or service. If the individual has missed the seminar, or has not returned to the afternoon presentation at your booth, it is even more important to write a follow-up letter.

General Rules

Be direct about the reason for the letter.
Summarize the major points of your product or service.
Stress the benefits your product/service can provide to the addressee.

Alternate Phrases

(a) I'm sorry that you couldn't make the color-graphics presentation after lunch at the Computer Color-Graphics Exhibit yesterday.

I missed you at the lecture given to your company by our representative last week.

It's too bad that you had to go out of town the morning of our scheduled seminar.

(b) Because of your obvious interest in the subject, I'm taking the liberty of writing to you and enclosing descriptive literature about our fine color-graphics desktop computer.

Since you arranged the lecture on "Management Requirement Planning" at your company, I thought you would like to get a printed copy of Robert Denning's presentation.

Since you indicated an interest in our popular seminar on "Dressing for Success," I'm writing you to let you know that on May 15 we will be giving the same seminar, at the same hall in your city.

(c) If you wish any further information, or if you want a demonstration of our product in your office, please let me know. The motto of our company is: "SERVICE WITH EXCELLENCE."

Again, sorry about your missing the presentation. If you want clarification of any point in the material, just give me a call.

Hope to see you at the May 15 seminar.

MATHEMATICA PRODUCTS GROUP

A DIVISION OF MATHEMATICA, INC.

P.O. BOX 2392

PRINCETON, NEW JERSEY

XXXXXXXXXXXXXX
XXXXXXXXXXXXXX
XXXXXXXXXXXXXX

Dear _____:

I'm sorry you were unable to join us at our recent RAMIS II sales seminar. Since you had indicated an interest in RAMIS II by registering for the seminar, I thought I would write to you to briefly acquaint you with our system.

RAMIS II is a proven, easy-to-use computer language with comprehensive capabilities for data base management, report preparation, and information retrieval.

Since its origin in 1967, RAMIS II has been expanded continually to include new features and benefits. These improvements have helped to simplify communications between the user and the computer. Users such as financial planners, marketing analysts, personnel administrators, as well as Management Information Systems and data processing staffs are represented among the more than 1,000 clients utilizing RAMIS II.

The enclosed material gives an overview of the RAMIS II system. Because we are convinced that RAMIS II is of genuine significance to the data processing industry, we ask that you give our brochures your special consideration. We believe it will be well worth your time.

A RAMIS II representative will phone within the next few days to answer any questions you may have.

Sincerely yours,

Vice President
U.S. Operations

Courtesy of Mathematica Products Group, Princeton, New Jersey

Follow-Up Sales Letter

• FOLLOW-THROUGH LETTER

A follow-through letter is an effective medium for keeping or getting back a customer or client as well as showing your continual interest in him or her. This section offers samples of follow-through letters. They are excellent guides to help you write your own letters. They also can be used as is—all you need to do is change pertinent data.

Dear Customer:

You don't want the fine cutting edge of your Marketing techniques to become dull, do you? You can, you know, become hopelessly out of date unless you are aware of the latest state-of-the-art in your dynamic profession.

You need the latest information about the volatile Marketing field; we supply that information to you. That is, we have supplied you with up-to-date news about trends, techniques, and people until last month, when you failed to renew your contract with us.

Stay with us. Stay sharp. Stay attuned to the changing scenery in the Marketing field. Renew your contract with **Marketing Services** today.

You and your company will be glad you did, and we will be appreciative.

Sincerely,

Director
Marketing Service

Dear Client:

Tell us what you think!

As a valued client, we'd like your opinion as to how we could improve the services our stock brokers provide to thousands of people like you.

Please take a few moments and check the list below. Additional comments or suggestions by you will be appreciated.

After completing the survey, please return it in the enclosed self-addressed, stamped envelope.

Thank you for your cooperation.

Sincerely,

FORTUNE RESEARCH DEPARTMENT

TIME INC., ROCKEFELLER CENTER

NEW YORK, N.Y. 10020

XXXXXXXXXXXXXX
XXXXXXXXXXXXXX
XXXXXXXXXXXXXX

Dear _____:

The bird is the fastest moving living creature. Speeds higher than 185 mph have been attributed to peregrine falcons.

Homo sapiens, of course, moves less quickly. But there is one group which is known for its remarkable mobility—the business executive.

For this reason, we ask you to take a moment now to review and update the information (printed on the enclosed card) that you were kind enough to provide us some time ago. The purpose of our continuing Subscriber Census is to make **Fortune** more relevant to the interests and responsibilities of our readers.

A postage-paid reply envelope is enclosed for your convenience. Please complete the card and drop it in the mail.

Many thanks for your cooperation.

Cordially,

Gail Clyma
Director
GC/vf
Enclosures

Through the courtesy of Fortune © *1979 Time Inc.*

Follow-Through Sales Letter

• GENERAL SALES LETTER

The objective of a good sales letter, like the purpose of any sales presentation, is to gain attention, hold interest, and to lead the potential customer to action.

General Rules

Stress "you" and "your" in the letter.

Emphasize the benefits the user can derive from your product or service.

Describe your product or service simply and accurately, so that it can be easily remembered.

Include testimonials, if possible.

Alternate Phrases

(a) Individuals who make fortunes in various investments always precede, never follow, the crowd. We are about to release a new 150-page *Guide* describing the most exciting opportunities of our time, where fantastic profits can be made by those who have the information on which to act.

I represent one of the world's largest life insurance companies and, in my opinion, the best. My business is cash value life insurance.

If you are planning to take a European vacation trip this year, we have a suggestion which can make this the best trip you ever made—and can save you money, too.

(b) This new compilation shows you how and where to invest in *new* coal and oil operations all over the U.S. to get the most profit.

As you might expect, there is more to the life insurance business than meets the eye. Basically, life insurance is to guarantee future payment of certain amounts of money at specified times, whether the person lives or dies. My job is to learn how such guarantees can contribute to my clients' financial well-being.

Our suggestion is that you rent a compact car through our agency here in the States, and pick up the car at your port of arrival. You can then see points of special interest without being tied to train or plane schedules. You will be able to come and go as you please. Moreover, because of our overseas affiliations, you will pay for gas at a discount price all through Western Europe.

(c) To obtain your first-press copy, with all the geographical, operational, and financial data, as well as names and addresses of where you can write for further information for sound and profitable investments, simply return the enclosed Reservation Card today.

Since my services might be of interest to you, I'd like to take a few minutes to tell you in more detail just what I do. I'll call you next week to arrange a convenient time.

We're looking forward to helping to make this the most interesting, relaxed, and economical trip you ever had.

ADDRESSOGRAPH-MULTIGRAPH CORPORATION

CLEVELAND, OHIO

Miss B.V. Davis, Principal
North High School
Winney Falls, Ohio

Dear Miss Davis:

Who was that man I seen you dancing with last night?

Pretty bad grammar, isn't it? If it were to appear on an English exam in your school, would it be legible enough for the students to read? One way to ensure that it can be read easily is to have the exams produced on a Multilith Offset Duplicator. Multilith Methods are widely accepted by business people the world over for their ability to reproduce clean, crisp copies at comparatively low cost.

With proven Multilith Methods, teachers can prepare their exams and quizzes directly on a paper master with pen, pencil or typewriter. Errors are easily erased and corrections made. From here on it's even easier. The master is placed on the duplicator where all the desired copies are produced. Moreover, another blank master can be run through the duplicator. This provides you with a duplicate master to file away for future use.

May I stop in to show you the high quality, simplicity, and economy of Multilith Offset Duplicator?

Sincerely yours,

C.A. Smith
Multigraph Representative
CAS:ny

General Sales Letter

• CONTACTING INACTIVE ACCOUNTS

The purpose of such a letter is to win back an old customer's patronage. Try to find out if he or she has a grievance. Once you know what the trouble is, you will be in a position to handle the rapprochement. The letters in this section will help you get this information and start the ball rolling toward a renewal of your old relationship.

General Rules

Tell the customer that his or her past orders or contracts have been appreciated.

Tell the customer how anxious you are to regain his or her account.

Ask why the company stopped doing business with you.

Assure the customer that you can serve him or her well.

Alternate Phrases

(a) It's hard to realize that it has been all of eight months since we've last received an order from you.

Just a short note to let you know that we have missed your coming into the place. The last time we saw you was just before Christmas.

We haven't heard from you for many months, and frankly we've missed you. An account as good as yours is hard to get, and we want you back.

(b) We were happy to have your account, and we certainly miss you. It would be a great pleasure to serve you again.

This is a matter of great importance to us because we very much want to keep old customers like you.

We want your business, and if there is anything that caused you to stop giving us your orders, we want to know what it is.

(c) Won't you use the back of this letter to tell us why you haven't been in to see us for such a long time? If there's any problem, we shall resolve it, so that our old relationship can resume.

Won't you please let me know personally why you have stopped placing orders with us? I would greatly appreciate it.

We are enclosing a self-addressed stamped envelope for your reply. We will appreciate this courtesy. Moreover, if it has anything to do with our personnel or procedures, you can rest assured that we will take action.

A.F. STALEY MANUFACTURING COMPANY

CORN AND SOYBEAN PRODUCTS

DECATUR, ILLINOIS

XXXXXXXXXXXXXX
XXXXXXXXXXXXXX
XXXXXXXXXXXXXX

Gentlemen:

We have missed you!

The fact is that the Company is deeply concerned when an excellent account, such as yours, fails to return to the "store."

It is our policy to handle our accounts with courtesy, understanding, and efficiency. Certainly, an account as important to us as yours is should have received this kind of treatment. Won't you, therefore, please tell us why you have stopped doing business with us?

Enclosed is a form and self-addressed stamped envelope for your frank comments.

Thank you.

Sincerely,

Credit Manager

Contacting Inactive Accounts

• THE PRE-APPROACH LETTER ASKING FOR AN INTERVIEW

A good letter can do more than just arrange a time and place for an appointment; it can sell the interview. If you word the letter skillfully, the prospect will not only expect you, but look forward to your visit.

General Rules

Keep the letter short and uncomplicated.

Use vigorous verbs instead of passive ones.

Hint at the benefits you can offer, but don't tip your hand. Save full description for the interview.

Ask for a definite appointment, or at least say you'll contact him or her by phone for one.

Alternate Phrases

(a) It's a fact: you will sell more accounting application packages to your customers by offering the "menu-ridden" Randy software.

Like similar companies everywhere, you can save time and money on every one of your jobs by using modern high-tension nut-and-bolt techniques where you now use rivets. Like to know how?

From the enclosed clipping it looks like your buying responsibilities have been expanded to include the purchase of inks and dyes.

(b) Because we have established quality commercial computer software packages, with emphasis on financial applications, this easy-to-sell product could substantially increase your sales volume.

This convenience can be yours at a surprisingly low cost.

To make your job easier, I would like to show you the complete line of top quality inks and dyes made by the Amir Company.

(c) Could I take thirty minutes sometime next week to explain what it is we offer? Of course, there's no obligation on your part.

You would get a much better idea from seeing it than from hearing about it.

There are several points I would like to explain.

(d) Would Thursday afternoon be all right, say about 3:30?

May I arrange an appointment for Wednesday morning to show it to you?

Since a demonstration is much better than a written or oral explanation, I will call you to set up an appointment at your convenience.

ADDRESSOGRAPH-MULTILITH CORPORATION

CLEVELAND, OHIO

XXXXXXXXXXXXXXX
XXXXXXXXXXXXXX
XXXXXXXXXXXXXX

Dear _____:

As a friend of A-M, we thought you would be interested in the attached literature about our latest office model.

Have you seen this highly efficient, cost beneficial A-M machine in action yet?

If you haven't, may I invite you to come to a demonstration as our guest next Friday? Let me know on the enclosed postcard if this is convenient for you.

Looking forward to seeing you, I am

Very truly yours,

The Pre-Approach Letter Asking for an Interview

• FOLLOW-UP AFTER PRESENTATION

A friendly letter of thanks for an interview or demonstration tends to reinforce the impact of the meeting, and helps to convince the prospect that he has been contacted by a well-run company.

General Rules

Thank the prospect for making the time available for the interview.
Summarize briefly your major selling points.
Emphasize your desire to do business with the prospect.

Alternate Phrases

(a)   Many thanks for taking the time in your busy schedule last week to discuss ways in which we may be able to serve you.

Thank you for the courtesy and consideration you gave me. It was very nice of you to take the time to discuss with me the possibility of setting up an account with my firm. I appreciate it.

I want to thank you for the courtesies you showed me during my recent visit with you. As you know, I have just been transferred to your territory and so I especially appreciate the friendly and attentive reception you gave me during our interview.

(b)   Since the selection of a computer system involves the consideration of many other factors besides benchmark performance, I'd like to point out several important advantages we can offer you.

With our wide range of products and technologies, we are confident that we can meet your requirements with devices uniquely suited to your exact needs. Our products are designed to provide you with better performance and significant cost-benefits.

We are equipped to give you as good a product and service as can be had in the business. In addition, we are in a position to offer you significant discount schedule. In short, we guarantee satisfaction.

(c)   We provide not only hardware and software, but also application programs tailored to your specific requirements. Moreover, we will train your staff to operate our IBC computer system efficiently and economically.

Feel free to call on me at any time that I can be of help to you. I am here to serve you.

I do hope that you will give some thought as to what type of arrangement we can set up. Could we perhaps discuss some ideas again soon?

GEORGIA-PACIFIC CORPORATION

EQUITABLE BUILDING

PORTLAND, OREGON

XXXXXXXXXXXXXXX
XXXXXXXXXXXXXXX
XXXXXXXXXXXXXXX

Dear _____ :

I tried to call you before leaving, but somehow I couldn't get connected. At any rate, it was a pleasure indeed to visit with you at breakfast. Your progress in this project is nothing less than fantastic.

I hope that we can work out a means of handling the plywood that you are developing for export once the mill is in operation.

My best wishes to you for completing your project successfully and within your schedule.

Best regards,

Follow-Up After Presentation

• INTRODUCING NEW SALESPERSON

A good letter of introduction can do such an effective job that the salesperson is welcomed when he or she appears at the customer's office or shop.

General Rules

Keep the tone of the letter informal.
Give the qualifications and background of the new individual.
Praise the sales person; express confidence in him or her.

Alternate Phrases

(a) We are pleased to introduce our new representative in your area, Miss Helen T. Baker. Helen has been brought up through the ranks, and she is now ready for an important assignment. She is an expert in our field, and can help you with any problem that might arise.

I'm dropping you a note to let you know that we have assigned Mr. George Arnold to your state as our representative. George is a specialist with valves, and can be relied upon to supply the best advice available.

The Range Company takes pleasure in introducing Mr. Jonathan T. Kingley. While his job will be to sell our products, his first obligation will be to analyze your specific requirements and make cost-effective recommendations.

(b) Helen has contributed much to the Company in each position she has held. Consequently, we are confident that she will do her usual outstanding job for you.

I don't know whether or not you are ready to buy our line right now. But you might be interested in hearing about the latest products and their cost-benefits in our field as they apply to your particular business.

A brief discussion with Mr. Kingley will convince you of his expertise of the field, and his down-to-earth approach to solving problems, we believe, will please you.

(c) We will appreciate any courtesy you show to her.

Could George call you within the next few days for an appointment?

Mr. Kingley is planning to visit you next Monday morning. If this is not convenient for you, or if you wish to speak to him sooner, please call our office.

AMERICAN VISCOSE CORPORATION

LOS ANGELES, CALIFORNIA

Film Division

To Our Business Friends:

It is a pleasure to announce that Mr. E. R. "Mike" Smith of our Technical Service Department will now work out of our Los Angeles office to give you prompt assistance with your packaging problems.

Mike, a specialist with cellophane for twenty-seven years, has had broad experience in production, quality control, technical service, film evaluation, and development. He is exceptionally well qualified to analyze problems and respond to your questions involving cellophane and packaging machinery, laminating, adhesives, and inks.

Now that Mike is with us, you will get even better service from Avisco on the West Coast.

Sincerely,

M.G. O'Connor
West Coast District Manager

Introducing New Salesperson

• ENCOURAGING SALESPERSONS

A letter encouraging the sales force is the most inexpensive way of asking for greater effort. Use it also to tell them that you have noticed and appreciated the effort they have made already towards furthering the company's success.

General Rules

Emphasize the important part salespersons play in your company's success.

Stress the positive; urge improvement of performance, for example, rather than dwell on faults.

Alternate Phrases

(a) While our figures are not yet complete, results are sufficiently conclusive to make it certain that the year just completed was an outstanding one. That this has been so is due in a very large measure to the extraordinary contributions that each one of you has made.

Another season has passed, and we have just finished taking stock of our assets and liabilities. We are most pleased to be able to tell you that our company is in excellent condition, and that the most important contributing factor has been the fine performance of our sales force. So please accept our sincere thanks for the wonderful job you have done.

A company such as ours is never any better than its salespersons. Judging by our past record, therefore, we have the best in both. I am sure you must be pleased to be part of such an excellent situation.

(b) There are valid reasons for believing that the year ahead will be just as successful. Industry demand continues strong. Popular acceptance of our products has never been higher. The most important asset our company has, however, is its people. It is your energy, your initiative, and your creative application to our challenging problems that will insure our continuing record of achievement.

There is every indication that the coming season can be better than the last one. Conditions throughout the country make this seem most likely. And you can help make this the most successful ever.

We know you realize that a company can only succeed if it continues to grow. To this end, we need and are sure we will get your best efforts.

(c) So, once again, thanks for your fine work. I am certain that similar thanks will be forthcoming next year.

We know you will do your best and we thank you for it.

We are certain it will be forthcoming, and we want to express our appreciation in advance.

GEORGIA-PACIFIC

To: _____

From: _____

Subject: National Salespersons' Week

This is National Salespersons' Week. We want, therefore, to recognize all of you for the important position you play in our company and in the economy of the nation as a whole. It is appropriate that the general public recognize your worthy profession.

Americans enjoy the highest standard of living in the world, not only because of our natural resources and our form of government, but because of our salespeople. You have carried the story of better living with sufficient effect to make mass production possible. This has broadened markets and created the real prosperity which America enjoys today.

We congratulate you on what you have done, and are happy to give you this recognition. We know you will meet the challenge of the 80's—a decade whose prosperity is once more dependent upon the effectiveness of America's sales force.

Encouraging Salespersons

8

Effective Credit and Collection Letters

The area of credit and collection is a delicate one in which all dealings require a firm but polite touch. Each letter you send should be designed for a specific function, and regardless of what that function is, each letter should fulfill it with dignity. Moreover, dignity should never be sacrificed for effect.

One of your most important needs in this area is a definite policy for extension of credit and collection of overdue bills. You probably have established already such a policy, and it includes the practice of checking the ratings and references of your potential credit customers. This gives rise to the need for the credit investigation letter. After the results of this letter are in, you will need either a letter granting credit or one refusing credit. Another widely used letter is one inviting charge accounts.

You will no doubt find that quite a few of your customers, businesses as well as individuals, have to be prodded into paying their bills. Some of them need but a gentle reminder; some must have several reminders; others won't pay until they receive an ultimatum. You will need collection letters for all of these contingencies. When to send these letters is a matter of company policy.

As to the letters themselves, those included in this chapter should cover most situations that you will be confronted with. All you need do is to turn to the page with the appropriate letter and use it exactly as is, or adapt it to your particular need. The difficult work of writing the letter has already been done for you.

• CREDIT INVESTIGATION LETTER

With only minor adjustments you can use the same letter to investigate the credit rating of an individual customer or the financial standing of a company.

General Rules

Come right to the point.
State what information you are looking for and why you need it.
Make clear that you will keep such information confidential.
Always enclose a self-addressed, stamped reply envelope.

Alternate Phrases

(a) Miss _____, whose residence is at _____, has applied for a loan with our company, and has given your name as a reference.

Please send us, at your earliest convenience, your annual statement for this year. We need such data to help us decide on the amount of credit we can extend to you.

We are in the process of gathering information about the financial responsibility of Mr. _____.

(b) We would appreciate your supplying us with any data that will help us evaluate Miss _____ as a credit risk. Information such as her reputation for reliability and her financial standing will be of utmost interest to us.

I'm sure you realize that we, operating primarily on a credit basis, need the latest financial reports of our potential customers.

It is our understanding that Mr. _____ has an account with your bank. Would you please send us whatever information you have relative to his ability to enter into a $10,000.00 transaction?

(c) Any information you send us will, of course, be held confidential. We enclose a reply envelope for your convenience.

Your financial reports will be held in the strictest confidence and used only to help us make our decision.

We appreciate your courtesy in supplying us with the needed data, and will, of course, treat them as confidential material. We are enclosing a reply envelope for your convenience.

JOUET INC. THE HOUSE OF PLAYTHINGS

346 CARROLL STREET

BROOKLYN, NEW YORK

XXXXXXXXXXXXXX
XXXXXXXXXXXXXX
XXXXXXXXXXXXXX

Dear _____:

The Apex Company, located at 6315 Broadway, has placed a $5000.00 order with us and has given your name as a reference.

Any information you can give us concerning this company's reputation for meeting financial obligations will be appreciated and, of course, held in strict confidence.

Thank you for your cooperation. If we can ever reciprocate, please call upon us.

Sincerely yours,

Enc: Self-addressed, stamped reply envelope.

Credit Investigation Letter

• LETTER GRANTING CREDIT TERMS

This is a pleasant letter to write. You are happily telling your customer that everything you have learned about him or her leads you to the conclusion that the person or company is a good credit risk. You are pleased and he or she will be, too.

General Rules

If you contacted his or her submitted references, tell the person so.

Tell the individual that you are looking forward to doing business with the company and/or him or her.

Offer the customer all the cooperation you can give.

Alternate Phrases

(a) As is our policy, we checked your references and were most pleased to learn of your excellent reputation in the financial community.

We contacted the references you submitted to us, and are pleased to inform you that all replies were more than satisfactory.

Your credit references have been contacted and their responses were most favorable.

(b) We are, therefore, very happy to grant you the loan you asked for to enlarge and remodel your store.

The Quality Company is pleased to extend to you our most favorable credit terms, 2/10 net 30, and looks forward to a long and mutually profitable association.

Therefore, we are extending to you the credit you asked for, and feel this is the beginning of a long and mutually beneficial relationship.

(c) We want to assure you that we will always be ready to help you in any way that we can, and will always be at your service.

It is a pleasure to be associated with a firm of your fine reputation, and you can rest assured that we will do our utmost to serve you satisfactorily.

It is our promise to contribute our share to achieve such a relationship.

K.B. DOLL CORPORATION

23 WEST 23RD STREET

NEW YORK, N.Y.

XXXXXXXXXXXXXXX
XXXXXXXXXXXXXX
XXXXXXXXXXXXXX

Dear Mr._____:

The credit references you provided us with have been contacted, and we are pleased to report that the replies are thoroughly satisfactory.

It is our pleasure to extend credit terms to you, and we can assure you of our cooperation at all times.

Thank you for choosing us to do business with. We have no doubt that our future business relationship will always be a source of satisfaction to both of us.

Very truly yours,

Letter Granting Credit Terms

• LETTER TURNING DOWN CREDIT APPLICANT

Turning down a credit applicant is an unpleasant task. But if you can write a tactful letter, you won't make the applicant hostile. A well-written letter can keep the applicant's business and goodwill, while a poorly written one will antagonize the person and will send him or her elsewhere.

General Rules

Thank the individual for his or her interest in your company.
Try in some way to soften the refusal.
Never tell the applicant he or she is a poor credit risk.
Always leave the door open for a future re-evaluation.

Alternate Phrases

(a) We very much appreciate your interest in opening a charge account with our company.

Thank you for your application for a credit account with our company.

(b) We regret that because we have received conflicting information, and because our credit resources have been taxed to their limit, we are unable to open a charge account for you at this particular time. We will be very happy to review your situation and ours in the near future, if you wish.

Based on information received, we do not feel that we are in a position to open an account for you at this time. If you feel that our action is not justified, or if you have information you believe we do not have, we would be very glad to review the entire matter with you.

(c) Until then, we look forward to seeing you and serving you to our very best ability, as we have in the past.

In the meantime, we hope that you will continue to enjoy our merchandise as you have these past two years.

EASTMAN KODAK COMPANY

ROCHESTER, NEW YORK

XXXXXXXXXXXXXX
XXXXXXXXXXXXX
XXXXXXXXXXXXX

Dear Ms Jones:

Thank you for your patience while we have been investigating your credit standing.

Unfortunately, the information we have obtained is not adequate for us to arrange credit accommodations for you at this time. We shall, of course, be happy to review your account later, if you wish, and we hope that terms may then be provided.

In the meantime, when you send us orders, won't you please enclose payment for them to prevent shipping delays?

Sincerely,

Letter Turning Down Credit Applicant

• LETTER OF SUGGESTION TO CUSTOMER

A customer who is having difficulty in making scheduled payments on a credit plan complicates your bookkeeping and adds to your overhead. A change in the type of credit account could ease the situation for both of you. You can suggest such a change with a tactful letter.

General Rules

Explain the situation to the customer.

Tell the customer what the unpaid and perhaps past due balance is. This will hammer home the need for the person to take your suggestion. (Sometimes it will motivate him or her to pay up the entire balance.)

Suggest the possibility that you may be in error, and invite the individual to correct the error.

Offer to change the account to one more suitable to him or her.

Alternate Phrases

(a) It has been our experience that sometimes it takes a little time to arrive at the best type of credit plan for a customer. We think that is the case in your situation. As you probably know, there is usually a balance in your account that exceeds the terms of our agreement. (The current balance is $_____.) Our financial advisers have studied your situation and think that you should have a _____ account.

Many customers find that their situation changes from the time they first open a charge account, and that they can no longer meet their obligations under the original agreement. In such cases we recommend a change of plan. Since your balance has remained at $_____ for some time now, we recommend that you consider a _____ type plan.

(b) If you don't agree with the conclusion we have reached, please let us know. We will be happy to consider any suggestion you may have. If we are in error, we would appreciate your pointing it out.

Our decision is not final; we always take our customers' opinions into consideration. So please get in touch with us.

(c) If you feel that a frank, face-to-face discussion would be more suitable to you, please call us. We would be happy to arrange a meeting at your convenience.

Please let us hear from you soon so that we can make mutually satisfactory arrangements.

We are at your service not only as credit personnel but also as financial advisers. In this regard, we would be most happy to discuss your situation with you and give any help we can.

JOHN WANAMAKER, PHILADELPHIA

INCORPORATED

PHILADELPHIA, PA

XXXXXXXXXXXXXXX
XXXXXXXXXXXXXX
XXXXXXXXXXXXXX

Dear Ms Williams:

In reviewing our records we find that your account often exceeds our terms of sales and now has a past due balance of $1,855.00. It may be that the regular thirty-day revolving credit plan is not the type best suited to your needs.

If our records are in error, we would appreciate hearing from you so that we may correct any mistake on our part.

If you feel that a different type of account would be more suitable, we will be happy to discuss the matter with you at your convenience.

Cordially yours,

Collection Department
John Wanamaker, Inc.

Letter of Suggestion to Customer

• REFUSING LOAN OR SPECIAL CREDIT TERMS

When you must refuse a loan or special credit terms to a customer, do so in a straightforward manner. Tell the customer exactly why you cannot grant his or her request.

General Rules

Use a friendly introductory paragraph to soften the refusal.

Be tactful in refusing the loan or special terms requested.

Never tell the customer his or her account doesn't warrant a loan or special terms.

If possible, suggest an alternative to meet his or her needs.

Alternate Phrases

(a) It gives us a great satisfaction whenever one of our customers calls upon us to solve a problem, and we are able to assist him or her. However, there are times when we just can't help.

Thank you for your letter asking about a different type of credit arrangement. It is always good to hear from you.

(b) We would be happy to grant your request if we could. But the fact is that if we did it for you we would be duty-bound to give similar terms to our other customers. And we are in no position to do this.

Our policy of extending the same privileges to all our customers is part of our reputation. Granting your request would be the one exception. So while we would like to give you the special credit terms you ask for, we just cannot do it without spoiling our reputation.

(c) Many of our customers, who at first blush think they need special credit terms, find on closer examination that our standard credit arrangements can be made to fit their needs. Might I suggest a closer look at what our usual terms provide?

Perhaps a further review of your situation will reveal that our regular credit terms are adequate for your use.

(d) If you have any questions, please don't hesitate to get in touch with us.

If we have left any questions unanswered, please let us know and we will do our best to answer them.

INTERNATIONAL BANK

INTERNATIONAL PLAZA

CHICAGO, ILLINOIS

XXXXXXXXXXXXXX
XXXXXXXXXXXXXX
XXXXXXXXXXXXXX

Dear Mr. Anderson:

Thank you for your letter. We are pleased to learn of your company's expansion in the last six months.

We would be happy to grant you the loan requested if we could. The fact is, however, that for the size of loan you are requesting, it is the bank's policy to have collaterals. We certainly sympathize with your need for a larger computer system to process all your operations, but I'm sure you understand that we cannot go against our long-standing policy.

Perhaps you could ask a couple of local companies to be your collaterals. Or perhaps you could consider a medium or even a mini-computer system as a starter to automate your operations. For such an investment you would need a substantially smaller loan than you are requesting—a loan that we could grant you without collaterals.

It was good to hear from you. If you care to discuss any of my suggestions, I would be happy to set up an appointment at your convenience. Just give me a call.

Sincerely,

Credit Manager

Refusing Loan or Special Credit Terms

• LETTER INVITING USE OF CHARGE ACCOUNT

If you want a cash customer or a person with good credit ratings to open a charge account, simply ask him or her to do so without beating around the bush. A simple, friendly letter may do the selling job for you.

General Rules

Say something complimentary to the prospect, but be careful that it sounds sincere.

Invite the individual to open a charge account.

Tell him or her about the convenience of having a charge account.

Make it clear that it's very simple to open or use an account.

Alternate Phrases

(a) Every businessman seeks the patronage of good customers. We are pleased to say that we at Abrams consider you among the best.

You have every reason to be proud of your reputation for paying your bills promptly. This has given you an excellent credit rating.

(b) Consequently, we sincerely hope that you will open a charge account with us.

We are, therefore, inviting you to open an account with us.

(c) You will enjoy shopping in our store. Our merchandise and service are kept at the highest possible level and offered to you at the lowest possible price.

We look forward to serving you along with our many satisfied charge account customers. We consider this a select group, one which we hope you will join.

(d) We hope you will get in touch with us very soon. Our Credit Department is eager to serve you.

We are enclosing an application for your convenience. Won't you fill it in now?

BAMBERGER'S

NEW JERSEY

XXXXXXXXXXXXXXX
XXXXXXXXXXXXXX
XXXXXXXXXXXXXX

Dear Miss Epstein:

Bamberger's New Jersey welcomes you. In business since 1892, Bamberger's is equipped to handle your needs efficiently and courteously.

Our wide assortment of merchandise offers you choice items at considerable savings. Our decorators are at your service to help with home decorating problems. And you may even shop by phone; just call your local Teleservice number listed in the phone book.

For purchases of furniture, rugs, appliances, and other items of large amount, you may have our "Homemaker's Account" with no down payment and up to 18 months to pay. Please ask your salesperson to arrange this for you.

We hope you'll visit us soon and open a charge account with us.

Cordially,

Manager
Credit Department

Letter Inviting Use of Charge Account

• SERIES OF COLLECTION LETTERS

You can gear your letters to the four phases of the collection process: reminder, inquiry, appeal, and demand. Or, you can use a series of letters that start with a mild reminder and get progressively stronger in their demand for payment.

General Rules

Don't write any of these letters in anger. Be especially careful of your demand letter. Use a polite tone rather than a brusque one.

Come right to the point: ask for the payment of a specific sum.

Always accent the "you" and "your."

Space your letters at one to two week intervals.

Alternate Phrases

(a) Just a brief reminder that your account is now past due.

Many of us appreciate a reminder when our accounts become past due. If you haven't mailed your remittance, please do so as soon as you can. If you have already done so, thanks.

(b) If you have already taken care of it, please disregard this note.

Your cooperation will be appreciated.

(c) We call to your attention that the amount of $_____ is past due.

Just a reminder that you still owe a balance of $_____.

(d) We need your cooperation so that we can continue to give you the fine service you are accustomed to. So please mail your remittance today.

We have always had your cooperation in the past as you have had ours. Won't you, therefore, mail us your remittance now?

(e) You still have a balance outstanding of $_____.

We wish to direct your attention to your outstanding balance of $_____.

(f) Won't you please mail your long overdue remittance today?

Please mail your delinquent payment today so that you won't have to be bothered with any more request letters.

(g) While we can't understand your failure to respond to our previous letters concerning your past due account, we once again urge you to send us your remittance.

We are quite disappointed that you did not see fit to respond to our previous letters regarding your overdue account.

(h) We shall expect either your remittance, or some explanation from you for the delay.

Your cooperation is essential, so won't you please mail us your check for your past due account?

THE BLUM STORE

NEW YORK, N.Y.

(Letter No. 1)

XXXXXXXXXXXXXXX
XXXXXXXXXXXXXX
XXXXXXXXXXXXXX

Dear Mr. _____:

May we call your attention to your account which is now past due? If your remittance has already been sent, please disregard this note.

Your cooperation as well as your patronage is always appreciated.

Very truly yours,

(Letter No. 2)

Dear Mr. _____:

A review of your account indicates that the balance listed below is past due.

So that we may better serve you, will you please favor us with an early remittance?

Very truly yours,

(Letter No. 3)

Dear Mr. _____:

We wish to call your attention to your account amounting to $_____.

Won't you please send us your check for the amount that is past due?

Very truly yours,

Series of Collection Letters

(i) Usually one or two reminders of an overdue account are sufficient to bring in the payment. You, however, have ignored our letters.

You no doubt have received our recent letters requesting payment of your overdue account.

(j) Won't you please put a check in the return mail?

Won't you please put your reply in the return envelope we are enclosing for your convenience?

(k) You have ignored all the letters we have sent you requesting payment of your overdue account.

We have received no acknowledgement from you regarding our request that you pay up your account.

(l) We must insist that you delay no longer in sending us your check.

We urge you to send us a check to avoid any unpleasantness.

(m) This is the last in a series of letters we have sent you.

You have given us no reason for your failure to make payment of your overdue account.

(n) If we do not receive your check in the return mail, we are forced to turn your account over to ———————— for collection.

Unless we hear from you within five days, it will be our unpleasant duty to hand your account over to our collection agency.

(Letter No. 4)

Dear Mr. _____:

Since we have received no reply to our previous letters, and due to the length of time which has elapsed, we must request that you send us the amount for your long past due account by return mail.

Your attention to this matter will be appreciated.

Very truly yours,

(Letter No. 5)

Dear Mr. _____:

We wish to call your attention to our recent letter requesting immediate payment of your account.

Will you please extend us the courtesy of a reply?

Very truly yours,

(Letter No. 6)

Dear Mr. _____:

We still have not received any reply to our previous letters requesting payment of your delinquent account.

Therefore, to avoid any unpleasantness we must insist that you give this matter your prompt attention and send us your check by return mail.

Very truly yours,

(Letter No. 7)

Dear Mr. _____:

This is our final request for the payment of your account.

Unless we receive your full remittance by return mail, we shall be obliged to hand your account over to the Philadelphia Credit Bureau for collection.

Very truly yours,

Series of Collection Letters (continued)

• NOTICE OF DELINQUENCY

While the Notice of Delinquency appears to be an official document, it is, in fact, just another device you can use to collect your debt. Of course, the more official it looks, the more effective it is likely to be.

Your Notice should contain the customer's name, your name, the amount due, and the name of your collection agency. Often, the name of your collection agency is just the type of prodding needed to get the customer to pay the bill.

However, your series of collection letters can end with Letter No. 7. While that letter lacks the official appearance of the Notice of Delinquency, it has all the other ingredients of a final demand notice.

CONSUMER CREDIT DIVISION

Date _____

You owe $_____ which is long past due.

> Mr. Robert L. Langer
> 4355 Winona Road
> Amarillo, TX

Member _____

Address _____

Our contract with the Philadelphia Credit Bureau compels us to report all past due accounts with their COLLECTION DEPARTMENT.

You, of course, realize that this will jeopardize your credit standing in the community. To avoid this action, you must make settlement IN FULL AT ONCE.

Credit Is Money

Keep Your Credit Safe for Tomorrow

Pay Promptly

Notice of Delinquency

• COLLECTION LETTER TO OLD CUSTOMER

If you must send a collection letter to an old customer, make it a gracious one. This is a good way of telling the person that although you are asking him or her to pay an overdue bill, you still regard the individual as a valuable customer.

General Rules

Mention the good relationship you have always enjoyed.
Offer to help him or her, if you can.
Offer the person the opportunity to save face.
Express confidence that he or she will pay.

Alternate Phrases

(a) (This paragraph can be omitted.)

We have enjoyed a mutually beneficial relationship for many years now, and I, for one, certainly hope that it will continue.

Our good relationship has endured over the years because we have always been able to communicate with each other.

(b) May we call your attention to your account which is now past due? If your remittance has already been sent, please accept our thanks and disregard this note.

An audit by our accountant indicates that the balance of $_____ in your account is past due.

If your payment is late because of some difficulty you've run into, why not give us the opportunity to help you?

(c) (This paragraph can be omitted.)

So that we may better serve you, we need your cooperation. Will you, therefore, favor us with an early remittance?

Or, if you have just been too busy to pay your bills—and we all are at one time or another—won't you try to get to them soon? We would appreciate it.

(d) (This paragraph can be omitted.)

Your cooperation will help us give you prompt and efficient service.

We feel certain that you will put your payment in the mail immediately. So, accept our thanks.

MINUTE MAID COMPANY

ORLANDO, FLORIDA

XXXXXXXXXXXXXX
XXXXXXXXXXXXXX
XXXXXXXXXXXXXX

Gentlemen:

We have been doing business together for a long time and have developed a mutually satisfactory relationship. Consequently, I know you will understand that my motive is entirely friendly in writing this letter to you about something that has been giving me some concern.

Our Accounts Receivable records show that your payments are reaching us increasingly late. We have always appreciated your promptness in the past. It is, however, important to you and to us, that we continue receiving your payments according to our terms.

If you have some serious problems confronting you, if you will tell us about them, perhaps we can help. If, on the other hand, somebody in your office has been a little careless, will you please see that our account is given closer attention in the future?

I know you will accept our request in the spirit in which it is intended, and will work with us in your usual cooperative manner. Will you send us a check for the past due invoices as soon as possible?

Thank you.

Sincerely,

MINUTE MAID COMPANY
Credit Manager

Collection Letter to Old Customer

• LETTER APOLOGIZING FOR COLLECTION LETTER SENT IN ERROR

No matter how efficiently you run your operation, you are eventually going to send a collection notice to someone in error. Accept the fact that it is going to happen, and when it does, just send a letter of apology. You will find your customer quite understanding, if your apology is honest and sincere.

General Rules

Apologize but never grovel.
Make it sincere but brief.
Acknowledge the inconvenience caused to the customer.
Assure the customer of your efforts to avoid any future mistakes.

Alternate Phrases

(a) The collection notice you received was sent in error. We therefore wish to apologize. We recognize and appreciate your record of prompt payment.

We don't make many mistakes, but when we do they are whoppers. Your account is in good order, as always. So please accept our apology for the collection letter erroneously sent to you.

Guess what? We goofed! We sent a collection letter to a customer with the best kind of payment record. Please accept our sincere apology.

(b) We try our best to prevent mistakes, especially of this type. Nevertheless it happened, and we are sorry that you have been inconvenienced.

I assure you that we will take every precaution to make certain that this type of mistake does not occur again.

You are one of our most valued customers, and I assure you that every effort will be made to keep this type of error from happening again.

(c) (This paragraph may be omitted.)

If you can spare the time during your next visit to our store, please drop in at the Credit Department. I would like to apologize in person.

We hope to continue serving you with ever-increasing efficiency.

JOHN WANAMAKER, PHILADELPHIA

INCORPORATED

PHILADELPHIA, PA

XXXXXXXXXXXXXX
XXXXXXXXXXXXXX
XXXXXXXXXXXXXX

Dear Ms _____:

Please accept our sincere apology for the notice recently sent to you in error. Your account, as usual, is in perfect order.

We make every effort to prevent computer-generated mistakes, nevertheless, as efficient as our data processing staff are, they do err once in a great while.

I am sorry if you have been inconvenienced by our error.

Sincerely,

Collection Department

Letter Apologizing for Collection Letter Sent in Error

• UNEARNED DISCOUNT LETTER

Some of your customers are going to take an unearned discount at some time or other in your business relationships. Writing to them presents a problem. Though you have to deny them the unearned discount, you want to keep their friendship. The letters presented here will help you overcome any difficulties.

General Rules

Be firm without being curt.

Thank the customer for his payment. If he includes a letter of explanation, acknowledge it.

Explain your discount policy.

Always name the specific amount you expect to receive.

Alternate Phrases

(a) The business you have given us deserves our recognition and thanks. If that was the only consideration, we would be happy to forget the discount you erroneously deducted. But as you know, the purpose of the discount allowance would be defeated if we allowed unearned deductions.

Thank you for your check No. _____, in the amount of $_____. We note that a discount has been deducted from this payment despite the expiration of the discount period.

(b) Our business must adhere to our discount policy, which is 2% in ten days; full payment in thirty days. Any exception affects our costs, and is unfair to customers who do pay within ten days.

We would appreciate your sending an additional check in the amount of $_____ to cover the discount you deducted.

We are returning your check No. _____ and would appreciate your sending us another check for $_____, representing the full amount.

(c) We are sorry to see you miss the earning of our 2% cash discount, and we hope that you will take advantage of it on future invoices.

If you still have any questions about our discount policy, please phone or drop in to see me. I would be most happy to talk with you about it.

We are sorry that you missed out on our cash discount by such a short period of time. We would overlook it, but that wouldn't be fair to our customers who made a real effort to pay our bills within ten days.

MINUTE MAID COMPANY

ORLANDO, FLORIDA

XXXXXXXXXXXXXX
XXXXXXXXXXXXXX
XXXXXXXXXXXXXX

RE: UNEARNED DISCOUNT FOR $702.50

Gentlemen:

The premium of 2% cash discount is for early payment. Since we did not receive your check for our invoice #12576 until 30 days after the discount period expired, we cannot allow your deduction.

Our discount policy was adopted after considering every possibility of treating all our accounts equitably. To forgive one for oversight and not the others would go against our established policy and besides, it would not be fair.

Consequently, we shall appreciate your check for $702.50 representing the unearned discount.

Thank you.

Sincerely,

MINUTE MAID COMPANY
Credit Manager

Unearned Discount Letter

9

Tested Letters
That Work in
Community Activities

It goes with the executive "territory" to be involved in community affairs, either personally or as a representative of his or her company. Almost always, such activity includes writing letters. This is an added drain on your limited time, but these letters are important and deserve closer attention than they often get. When you are acting on behalf of your company, especially, your letters can have a bearing on the company's status in the community, a significant variable in today's business world.

Moreover, community letters saying "no" may be of more consequence than those saying "yes." Good deeds speak for themselves, but when you must refuse to contribute or to participate you need an appropriate, well-written letter.

This chapter contains sample letters covering typical situations that might confront you in connection with community affairs. These models will save you time and effort when you have community obligations to meet.

- **ACCEPTING AN INVITATION OR OFFERING TO AID COMMUNITY PROJECT**

Many executives help out in community activities by accepting an invitation, or by offering their time and expertise. The letter you write, whether in response or in offering to assist, is a goodwill ambassador on its own—or should be.

General Rules

Indicate your willingness to help the stated worthy cause.
Specify the exact nature or the area of expertise you can offer.

Alternate Phrases

(a) I am very pleased to accept your invitation to attend the charity fund in Princeton on December 3, 19— —.

I would like to attend the church bazaar in Sioux Falls on June 7, 19— —. Can you please tell me whom I should contact to get a couple of tickets?

Because I am quite impressed with your organization and the wonderful work you do, I would like to offer my assistance.

(b) As you know, I might be able to sell tickets for your charity fund. If you need help in this regard please call upon me. If not, perhaps I can be useful in some other task.

I'm pleased to tell you that my company is in a position to make concrete contributions to the success of your project. For example, we would be happy to make available to you our loudspeaker equipment.

My training and experience are in the area of publicity, and I may be able to contribute most along those lines. However, I will be happy to help you out in whatever work is needed.

(c) Please let me know when we can get together to discuss how I can contribute to the success of your charity fund.

Please give me a call if we here at the American Bank can be of assistance to you in any way.

Here are both my home and business telephone numbers so that you can contact me at your convenience.

APEX REALTY CO.

445 CARRIAGE HILL RD.
TARRYVILLE, VERMONT

XXXXXXXXXXXXXX
XXXXXXXXXXXXXX
XXXXXXXXXXXXXX

Dear Mr._____:

I'm pleased and honored to join the town's citizens who are participating in the Mayor's campaign to fight juvenile delinquency through affirmative action.

I have always been interested in this problem, and I am happy to accept your invitation to work with the Mayor. I hope I can make some meaningful contribution to the success of this worthwhile project.

Thank you for inviting me to the very first meeting. I will be there. If I can be of any assistance before the meeting, please let me know.

Sincerely,

**Accepting an Invitation or Offering
to Aid Community Project**

• INVITATION TO OPEN HOUSE OR SIMILAR EVENT

Sooner or later your company is likely to hold an open house, a dedication ceremony, or some other function to which clients as well as well-known people in the community are invited. The right letter can create a feeling of goodwill, regardless of whether the people accept or decline the invitation. The letter, like the occasion, should be informal, projecting warmth and friendliness. If you feel that the occasion calls for more than an informal letter, you can use a card like the one shown here.

The Printed or Engraved Invitation

The Officers and Directors

of The First National Bank of Washington cordially invite you
to a private showing of their new building Saturday, the ninth of December,
from four until six o'clock

1701 Pennsylvania Avenue, N.W.
Washington, D.C.

General Rules

Be enthusiastic yet informal in describing the event, so the reader will want to come.

Be warm in your welcome.

Give details of time and place

Alternate Phrases

(a) You are cordially invited to attend the open house and reception on March 7, from 1:00 to 4:00 p.m. in the ABC cafeteria. Refreshments will be served.

The Union Company is pleased to invite you and your family to an open house on July 1, from 9:00 to 11:00 a.m. in our main building. Refreshments will be served.

(b) We would like you to join us in celebrating our 50th anniversary. We hope to share this joyous occasion with as many members of our fine community as possible.

We have sponsored the Art Festival for many years. And we are very pleased at the number of people from the community as well as our employees who always come and enjoy this annual event. This year, to make the occasion even more pleasant, we have added a musical trio that will play appropriate music.

(c) We look forward to seeing you again.

We hope you can be with us on this happy occasion.

PRENTICE-HALL, INC.

ENGLEWOOD CLIFFS, NEW JERSEY

XXXXXXXXXXXXXX
XXXXXXXXXXXXXX
XXXXXXXXXXXXXX

Dear Mr._____:

You are cordially invited to attend our annual Spring Art Festival. The showing will take place in the Prentice-Hall cafeteria from 5 to 7 p.m. on Monday, May 28. Refreshments will be served.

It has long been our practice to sponsor a continuing program of art appreciation for the enjoyment of our employees and visitors. Now for the first time our employees will have the opportunity to display their creative talents along with our art collection.

During the past several years, the Prentice-Hall art collection has grown to include examples of many different schools of painting from many countries. In addition, through the courtesy of various individual art collectors, artists, and galleries, numerous works have been loaned to us for exhibition.

We believe you will enjoy yourself, and we are looking forward to your visit.

Cordially,

RSVP

Invitation to Open House or Similar Event

• CONTRIBUTING TO CHARITY

You will probably want to communicate with charities by letter. This arrangement serves a threefold purpose: (1) It gives you enough time to find out if a bona fide organization is making the request; (2) it gives you a record to refer to from year to year in continuing or discontinuing your contribution; and (3) it gives you a handy reference for income tax purposes, i.e., in addition to your canceled checks.

General Rules

Praise the charity organization, and the work being done by the people associated with it.

Don't dwell on the amount of the donation.

Make it clear whether it's the company or you, personally, who is making the contribution.

Alternate Phrases

(a) For many years I have followed with interest the work you have been doing in behalf of the Cancer Fund.

We are happy to add the Heart Fund to our company list of charitable organizations to which we regularly contribute.

I have been interested in the young people and their problems for a long time, and I welcome the opportunity to help your worthy organization.

(b) I appreciate your giving me the opportunity to contribute to such a worthwhile cause.

Our top management feels that this is the least we can do when people like yourself do so much.

Both my company and me are pleased to contribute to such worthy community projects.

(c) Enclosed please find my check for $_____ to be used for the Cancer Fund. The best of luck to you and your organization.

Attached please find our check for $_____. You can count on us for continuous support of the Heart Fund.

Here's our check for $_____. Best wishes for the success of your project.

TRANSIT FREIGHT CO.

3900 JUNIPER AVENUE
KINGSTON, NEW YORK

XXXXXXXXXXXXXX
XXXXXXXXXXXXXX
XXXXXXXXXXXXXX

Dear Mr. Johnson:

We found your letter and the accompanying literature about the Niagara Disabled Young Artists both touching and impressive.

We will be happy to contribute to this worthwhile cause and add it to our list of charitable organizations. For now, enclosed please find our check for $_____.

We certainly wish you the best of luck in your endeavor to have these young artists realize their full potential and become self-sufficient.

Sincerely,

Contributing to Charity

• REFUSING CONTRIBUTION TO CHARITY

This is probably one of the most difficult letters that you will be called upon to write. Most charities perform a much-needed service for the community and deserve cooperation. However, it is impossible for an individual or even a large corporation to contribute to all these fine groups. Your refusal need not be construed as a lack of sympathy for the cause. Here is where a tactful letter can help.

General Rules

Praise the cause or the project they are working on.
Wish them every success in their drive.

Alternate Phrases

(a) I'm sorry to say that I cannot contribute to your fine organization.

I sincerely regret that I have to decline your request for a donation at present.

I'm sorry to tell you that our company cannot make its usual contribution to your most worthwhile organization.

(b) I support many charities in our community. However, as you must realize, I couldn't possibly contribute to all of them.

I have already gone over my quota for charitable contributions for this year.

Our budget does not permit any further contributions for this year. We hope that you will understand the necessity for a business to operate within its budget even when so fine a cause as yours is concerned.

(c) I sincerely wish you well in finding funds to continue your activities.

I have long admired the splendid work you do in our community and wish you every success.

Though we can only wish you well this year, perhaps next year we will be in a position to contribute generously to the outstanding work you do.

NATIONWIDE HOTEL CORP.

800 REGENT BOULEVARD

RAMSHEAD, PENNSYLVANIA

XXXXXXXXXXXXXX
XXXXXXXXXXXXXX
XXXXXXXXXXXXXX

Dear Ms_____:

We have carefully considered your request for a contribution to the Third Inter-American Musical Festival. We fully agree with you, we should strengthen our cultural ties with Latin America, our neighbors down south.

We would like to respond affirmatively to all the appeals we receive, however, our charity funds are limited. Moreover, since our operations are domestic, it is our policy to concentrate our support activities in the areas of community chests and aid for education, particularly in the localities where we have our major facilities.

We are sorry that we cannot contribute to the Festival, but wish you every success with your worthy project.

Sincerely,

Refusing Contribution to Charity

• REFUSAL TO AID COMMUNITY PROJECT

If you don't want to, or cannot accept an invitation to help on a community project, send a sincere, courteous letter of declination.

General Rules

Compliment the person on the work done by the individual and the organization.

Be sincere when you say that you would help the project, if it were possible.

Leave the door open for future participation or other form of help.

Alternate Phrases

(a) You and your organization should get an accolade for the devotion with which you carry out the desperately needed work for the local SPCA. I wish I were in a position to accept your invitation to join you and become a board member, but unfortunately I'm not.

I have long admired the contribution you and your organization make to the community. The Vocation Center for the Handicapped is a most worthwhile project, and if circumstances were different it would be a pleasure for me to join your organization.

Because of the work you and your organization do, ours is a safer community. Ordinarily, I would jump at the opportunity to join you. Unfortunately, previous commitments make it impossible for me to do so at present.

(b) I am on the board of several equally worthwhile organizations, and there is just not enough time for me to take on another one.

Because all of my spare time and energy are devoted to the Charities project, it is quite impossible for me at present to get involved with any other project.

I'm sure you will understand that because I'm so active in behalf of the Heart Fund, no time is left for me to join your project.

(c) Thanks for your invitation. Perhaps we can get together sometime in the future.

Please call on me in the future, as by then I may be able to join your organization.

The best of luck for the success of your project.

PREMIER ELECTRICAL CO.

455 GAINSBORO AVENUE
TALUSA, SOUTH CAROLINA

XXXXXXXXXXXXXX
XXXXXXXXXXXXXX
XXXXXXXXXXXXXX

Dear Mrs._____:

Your outstanding work in behalf of senior citizens in our community is well known.

Under different circumstances I would be happy to accept your invitation to join your admirable group.

I am, however, deeply involved in trying to improve the lot of children with muscular dystrophy. If I were to take on additional responsibilities in any other cause, I couldn't possibly do a good job in either community project.

I know you will understand the position I am in, and if there's any other way I can be of assistance, please call me.

Best of luck in your project, and thanks again for inviting me.

Sincerely,

Refusal to Aid Community Project

• REQUESTING CHANGE IN ZONING LAWS

The letter you write asking for a change in zoning laws will most likely go to a local board already swamped with similar requests. If you state your case clearly and simply, yet graciously, you will increase your chances of getting your request.

General Rules

Make your letter as concise and technically correct as possible.
Come right to the point. Tell the board why you need the change.
Indicate how the change will benefit the community, if appropriate.
Be courteous.

Alternate Phrases

(a) I hereby request a change in zoning of Parcel 216/31 from R-2 to R-5-A.

The Retro Company respectfully requests that C-3-B district in square 75 be extended to include lots 802 through 807 inclusive. The said property is located on the north side of I Street, and further identified as 2105 through 2119 I Street, inclusive.

On behalf of Simona & Co., it is respectfully requested that a public hearing be granted to consider an application for the extension of C-4 District to embrace the north and south side of F Street.

(b) The above parcel and the three parcels to the east, for which a similar request for change in zoning will be made, is entirely unimproved and is surrounded by Suitland Parkway, the Garfield School grounds, and property zoned R-5-A.

To utilize this very valuable site to its fullest potential and to erect a building, which will not only be a credit to the company but will be a landmark in the community, it is necessary to seek an extension of the business zoning to cover the entire site in question.

(c) (This paragraph may be omitted.)

Thank you for your consideration. I really appreciate it.

For the reasons stated above, and additional reasons to be presented, we respectfully urge that the Zoning Commission grant a public hearing to consider our request.

APEX REALTY COMPANY

445 CARRIAGE HILL ROAD

TARRYVILLE, VERMONT

XXXXXXXXXXXXXX
XXXXXXXXXXXXXX
XXXXXXXXXXXXXX

RE: CHANGE IN ZONING LAW

Gentlemen:

The undersigned are owners of Lot 16 in Square 3351, improved by premises 7056 Eastern Avenue, N.W.

Currently the front part of our property is zoned R-5-A, while the rear portion is zoned C-M-1. As the C-M-1 area has no street frontage, it is accessible only across the R-5-A area.

Under these conditions, and since several apartment buildings have recently been erected in this block, we feel the property can best be developed for apartment house use in its entirety. Consequently, we request that the whole lot be zoned R-5-A.

Thanking you for your early attention to this request, we are

Very truly yours,

Requesting Change in Zoning Laws

10

Responsible Letters to the Media

Executives, being individuals with certain philosophies and opinions, there will be occasions when a large number of you will strongly agree *or* disagree with an article or item you have read or heard on the TV or radio. Admittedly, writing effective letters to the local or national press, TV or radio news, or documentary programs to congratulate, criticize, make a point, or take a position on something is not the easiest task. But if you feel strongly enough about it, you will want to do it. More importantly, the correcting of certain misinformation or false data about your company that appeared in print or was broadcast is part of your responsibility as an executive.

Moreover, your letters to the media, especially when you're speaking for the Company, give an impression about your company that can have a significant impact on the public. In short, it is very important that your letters to the media be effective, well written, and appropriate.

This section offers examples of letters written by executives to the media on various topics. They are excellent guides to give you ideas on how to organize and present different subjects, and help you write your own letters.

NATIONAL ASSOCIATION OF RETIRED FEDERAL EMPLOYEES

1533 NEW HAMPSHIRE AVE.

N.W. WASHINGTON, D.C. 20036

Joseph E. Oglesby
Director of Public Relations

May 5, 1981

Dear Editor:

    Your April 28 editorial entitled "Pensions and Superpensions" contained many misleading elements which can only serve to prejudice the public against those Federal employees who serve the public.

1. It is indeed possible that in a period of sustained high inflation a retiree whose annuity is pegged to inflation can earn more in retirement than he once received in salary—whether it is a high-paid Congressman or a low-paid messenger. This is more of a commentary on inflation than a valid criticism of indexing, for the purpose of indexing is to protect the buying power of the original annuity—no more and no less.

2. By singling out Congressmen and the highest-paid members of the Executive Branch, you unwittingly imply that ALL Federal retirees are receiving $60,000 or more per year, when in fact the AVERAGE Federal civilian retiree receives $9540 per year, and the average survivor annuitant receives $4032 per year according to the latest data published by the agency that administers the retirement program.

3. You implied that twice-a-year inflation adjustments overcompensate Federal retirees. An official of the General Accounting Office has testified to Congress that they do NOT. In other words, the adjustment formula washes out the element of compounding.

4. Finally, you quoted Congresswoman Oaker as saying that twice-a-year adjustments are an "easy target." We would suggest that they have been made a "very VISIBLE" target by editorials such as yours.

Sincerely,

Joseph E. Oglesby

Letter Correcting Misinformation

GREATER WOODSIDE BUSINESS ASSOCIATION

WOODSIDE, OREGON

XXXXXXXXXXXXXX
XXXXXXXXXXXXXX
XXXXXXXXXXXXXX

Dear Editor:

Representing the firms in this area, I'm writing to you concerning the fire protection in the Woodside community where voters rejected a special tax levy. I can sympathize with the voters for not wanting additional taxes, but at the same time how can voters expect the Woodside firemen to do their job efficiently when they have to close down a fire station and lay off ten people because of lack of funds? Last week, within a 26-hour period, there were four structure fires, one resulting in the total loss of a printing shop.

It is my hope that the Woodside firemen do not take the recent rejection of the special tax as a barometer of the public's gratitude. It's too bad that people don't give much thought to their fire department until their house, or store, or business facility is on fire.

We, at the Greater Woodside Business Association, are very proud and most appreciative of our firemen. And in our opinion they deserve the community's thanks and full support.

Sincerely,

Jeff Hansen
President

Letter Taking a Position

CALIFORNIA STATE AUTOMOBILE ASSOCIATION

150 VAN NESS AVENUE

SAN FRANCISCO, CALIFORNIA 94101

XXXXXXXXXXXXXXX
XXXXXXXXXXXXXXX
XXXXXXXXXXXXXXX

Dear Editor:

I read with interest your editorial in yesterday's paper on "The Tax on Gasoline."

The California State Automobile Association suggests another approach which does not involve increasing taxes and fees. That approach is to use the windfall revenues accruing to the general fund from the sales tax on gasoline. This tax should not be confused with the 7¢ per gallon state tax on gasoline.

When the sales tax was imposed on gasoline in 1972, it was for the specific purpose of raising revenue for transportation purposes. Since then, the cost of gasoline has increased dramatically, as has the revenue from the sales tax.

The net result is that some $460 million per year more is being collected from this source than is being allocated for transportation purposes.

If this windfall was used for transportation, no deficit would develop and there would be no need to increase taxes on motorists.

Sincerely,

R.V. Patton
President

Through the courtesy of R.V. Patton, California State Automobile Association, San Francisco, CA.

Letter Making a Point

REEDS COMPANY

EVANSVILLE, ILLINOIS

XXXXXXXXXXXXXX
XXXXXXXXXXXXXX
XXXXXXXXXXXXXX

Dear Sir:

We here at Reeds Company are highly disturbed about a part of your news broadcast last night in which you stated that the "Executive Vice-President of Reeds Company, Evansville, Ill., James Derek, has been indicted for tax evasion."

Mr. Derek does NOT work for Reeds Company of Evansville: he works for Reeds Corporation of Chicago. There's NO connection whatsoever between these two firms.

We are looking forward to the retraction of the above item as soon as possible in your regular evening news broadcast.

Yours truly,

William Hanley
Executive Vice-President

Letter Demanding Retraction

CALIFORNIA TEACHERS ASSOCIATION

1705 MURCHISON DRIVE

BURLINGAME, CALIFORNIA 94010

XXXXXXXXXXXXXX
XXXXXXXXXXXXX
XXXXXXXXXXXXXX

Dear Editor:

In a recent commentary, "Disciplining Teachers," your associate editor observed that criticizing schools and complaining about teachers seems to be "increasingly fashionable." He is uncomfortably correct, but it's a myth that our schools are failing.

Today we have more boys and girls finishing high school than ever—over 75 percent of our youth. About half go to college. More blacks and Hispanics, as well as students with physical limitations, are finishing school.

In California our assessment program shows excellent gains, except for the 12th grade. Recently, the National Assessment of Education Progress reported gains in all grades except the latter part of high school. Young blacks were reported substantially better than a decade ago. The problem at the high school level is not with the basics but in the ability of students to reason and think critically, according to the report.

Your associate editor noted in his column "deep frustrations" about public schools are resulting in attempts to discipline teachers. The targets are gains won by teachers over the years, such as due-process evaluation and dismissal, improved salaries and working conditions, and being involved in decisions affecting the classroom through collective bargaining.

This is frightening because it's an emotional response to deep frustrations. Such emotional responses generally result in half-baked solutions or in punishing scapegoats, such as teachers, and usually are off-target.

Through the courtesy of Ed Foglia, California Teachers Association, Burlingame, CA.

Letter Providing Constructive Criticism

Yes, the schools have problems. We have too many kids who need special help so they can grapple with space-age academic demands. But our No. 1 problem is not in the classroom. It's this "fashionable" negative criticism of schools and teachers based on myth, not fact. The schools need public support and positive, not punitive, approaches to their problems.

Sincerely,

Ed Foglia
President

Letter Providing Constructive Criticism (continued)

PLEASANTVILLE CHAMBER OF COMMERCE

PLEASANTVILLE, IDAHO

XXXXXXXXXXXXXX
XXXXXXXXXXXXXX
XXXXXXXXXXXXXX

Dear _____:

I must congratulate you for taking a strong stand on the "No Growth" environmental issue in your morning radio news show.

The residents of Pleasantville join you in wanting to keep our town the way it is; the way it has been for the past 25 years: peaceful and beautiful.

We don't want a deluge of track houses and shopping centers that would inevitably follow the location of a large electronics company. The building of such facilities might mean riches to certain individuals, but to the rest of us in Pleasantville this would mean a sharp increase in traffic, pollution, and crime.

We are most appreciative of your bringing our "cause" to the public's attention.

Sincerely,

Alan Ramsey
Executive Director

Letter of Congratulation

11

Courteous Letters to Gain Employee Cooperation

There are many occasions when only a personal letter to an employee will get the goodwill management wants to effect. Some companies that rely on other channels of communications such as memos or announcements, overlook the fact that a personal letter can often succeed where other methods fail.

For best results, a letter from management to an employee should refer to a specific event or situation in which he or she has been or will be involved. For example, you can thank your employee by letter for submitting a suggestion, you can congratulate your employee by letter for a well-earned promotion, or you can use a letter to announce a new employee benefit plan. This type of letter, signed by an officer of the company, helps build cooperation and boosts morale within the organization.

For maximum effectiveness, letters to employees should be sent to their homes and not distributed at the office or factory. The letter so received will be more appreciated by the employee than one given to him or her at the facility. The person will feel that the company regards him or her as an individual and will respond by being a better employee.

The examples in this chapter show you how successfully a letter to employees can be handled.

• WELCOMING A NEW EMPLOYEE

Sometimes you might welcome a new employee by telephone or in person, but most of the time you will use a letter. Such a letter serves a double purpose. You not only welcome a new employee but you also confirm the individual's title, salary, the major fringe benefits, and other factors that were discussed in person or by telephone. This practice will minimize the possibility of any misunderstanding.

General Rules

Give all the pertinent information.

If there is any special arrangement, as in the sample letter, make certain you explain it clearly.

Make this a goodwill letter by expressing your pleasure at his/her accepting employment with your company.

Alternate Phrases

(a) It is a pleasure to welcome you as a new member of the Ebe Company. You are now a part of one of the world's largest publishers of books and information services.

On January 15, 19— —, at 9:00 a.m. please report for work at the personnel office of Value House, Inc. We hope you are looking forward to this event as enthusiastically as we are.

On February 1, 19— —, at 9:00 a.m., your career at The MIR Electronics Company will begin. We welcome you with great pleasure.

(b) You are now a member of a fine group of people operating as a team with the common objective of providing the finest books and business services in the world today.

As you become more familiar with your assignment and better acquainted with the other staff, you will find that all of us have an important part in producing quality merchandise.

We are confident that your coming on board will be the start of a mutually rewarding relationship.

(c) My warmest wishes to you in your new position with the Ebe Company. The welcome mat is out for you.

We are very happy that you have chosen Value House for your career. We look forward to seeing you.

So again, welcome. If you have any questions, please let us know.

K. B. DOLL CORPORATION

346 CARROLL STREET

BROOKLYN, NEW YORK

XXXXXXXXXXXXXXX
XXXXXXXXXXXXXX
XXXXXXXXXXXXXX

Dear Mr._____:

I want to welcome you to our firm. We are very pleased that you have accepted our employment offer and are looking forward to seeing you at our offices in two weeks, on February 1.

As we stated in our employment offer, it is the company policy to pay for our professional staffs' moving and travel expenses. The transportation company under contract to us will get in touch with you to move all your household goods. Your personal transportation expenses will be paid by us at the time you report for work.

Again, welcome to K.B. Doll Corporation. We are happy you have decided to join our organization, and we are confident that both you and our firm will benefit from this association.

Sincerely,

Welcoming a New Employee

• TURNING DOWN JOB APPLICANT

The applicant you must turn down today may be a needed employee tomorrow. You can turn him or her down and still leave the individual with a good impression of your company by writing a courteous and encouraging letter. It's nothing more than good public relations.

General Rules

Thank the applicant for considering employment by your firm.
Tell the person that you seriously considered his/her application.
Don't say that he/she lacks the proper training or experience.
Keep the tone of the letter positive.

Alternate Phrases

(a) Thank you for your letter and resume in response to our ad in the Sunday papers.

Thank you for your letter in which you expressed interest in editorial work with the Roger Company.

(b) Your qualifications have been reviewed carefully in the light of our current needs, and I regret to say that at this time we do not have an appropriate opening for a person with your background and experience.

We regret to inform you that at the moment no suitable vacancies exist for which you can be considered. However, if our requirements should change in the near future, we shall most certainly contact you.

(c) With your fine background and qualifications I am sure you will have no problem finding the right position.

Thank you for your interest in our company, and may I take this opportunity to wish you the best of luck in your search for new employment.

KAISER INDUSTRIES CORPORATION

300 LAKESIDE DRIVE

OAKLAND, CALIFORNIA

XXXXXXXXXXXXXX
XXXXXXXXXXXXX
XXXXXXXXXXXXXX

Dear _____ :

Thank you for your recent inquiry regarding employment with Kaiser Industries Corporation.

We have reviewed your qualifications with the various Kaiser affiliated companies and regret to report that we do not at this time have an appropriate vacancy. We are, however, taking the liberty of retaining your resume in our active files in the event of future openings in your field.

Your interest in our organization is very much appreciated, and we sincerely hope that we will be in a position to offer you more encouragement at a later date.

Yours very truly,

Turning Down Job Applicant

• INFORMING AN EMPLOYEE OF PROMOTION

This is a pleasant letter to write. It should be a joy to write and a joy to receive.

General Rules

Make the letter warm and sincere.
Keep the tone of the letter informal.

Alternate Phrases

(a) I'm very happy to tell you that your promotion to Computer Operations Manager has come through.

Congratulations! You have been promoted to Western Regional Sales Director.

(b) You certainly deserve this promotion since you have worked long and hard to make our computer operations run efficiently.

I don't have to tell you how proud we all are of you and your outstanding sales record, and of course, your promotion.

(c) Congratulations, Mark, and the best of luck to you in your new position.

Again, the best of everything in your new job.

AMERICAN VISCOSE CORPORATION

6333 EAST CORSAIR STREET

LOS ANGELES, CALIFORNIA

XXXXXXXXXXXXXX
XXXXXXXXXXXXXX
XXXXXXXXXXXXXX

Dear Bob:

It is with great pleasure that I inform you that the Board of Directors voted to promote you to the position of Vice President, Marketing Division.

There isn't another person that I know who deserves this promotion more than you do. Your efforts these past few years have contributed substantially to the success of our company.

Congratulations, Bob. You really earned this promotion.

Warmly,

Informing an Employee of Promotion

• INVITING EMPLOYEES TO MAKE SUGGESTIONS

Your employees can be the best source of ideas for improving company operations. A suggestion program, however, can bog down unless you consistently urge employees to use it. A letter can be the reminder they need, and it can also serve to introduce the plan to a new employee.

General Rules

Invite the employee to participate.
Make the letter friendly and warm.
If an award is involved, tell him or her how the amount is arrived at.
Tell the employee how he/she as well as the company benefits from good suggestions.

Alternate Phrases

(a) We have a suggestion box near you; all you need to do is make your suggestion and drop it in the box. Be sure to include your name and department.

Our Suggestion Program is very simple. You write down an idea you have to improve any phase of our manufacturing, then give your suggestion to your immediate superior and he will see to it that it gets to the Evaluating Committee.

(b) For each company-improving idea you submit, you will earn ten dollars.

If your suggestion is accepted, you will receive an award based on its value to the company. This decision will be made by the Evaluating Committee.

(c) Look around your department. Ask yourself: Is there a less expensive way of doing any of the work? Is there a way to improve the quality and accuracy of any of the processes? If you come up with an idea, send it in. We need your suggestions.

EASTMAN KODAK COMPANY

ROCHESTER, NEW YORK

XXXXXXXXXXXXXXX
XXXXXXXXXXXXXX
XXXXXXXXXXXXXX

Dear Mary:

Are you familiar with our Suggestion Plan?

We have put brightly painted boxes on each floor marked "Suggestions" and some blank paper for any idea you think has merit.

The idea may be one to reduce costs, to improve the quality of any of our products, or to make a desirable change in some method or procedure, or any other suggestion.

If any of your recommendations are approved, you get an award according to the value of the idea.

The Suggestion Plan is one of the best mediums for expressing your interest, your ingenuity, and your initiative. Simply fill out a blank paper by the "Suggestions" box and send it to our office by inter-office mail. Your idea will receive prompt acknowledgement and investigation and, we hope, an approval and award.

Sincerely,

Suggestion Office

Inviting Employees to Make Suggestions

• THANKS FOR VALUABLE SUGGESTION OR INFORMATION

Sending a letter of appreciation to an employee for a suggestion or information is one of the most inexpensive yet effective ways of encouraging the individual to continue to show interest in the company's operations. Thank him or her even if you don't use the particular suggestion or information.

General Rules

Mention the actual suggestion or information in the letter.

If used, state how the suggestion will help the company. If not used, hold out the possibility of future reconsideration.

Express your appreciation freely.

State how the submitted suggestion or information will help the employee.

Alternate Phrases

(a) Your suggestion concerning the replacement of the lug nuts used on tire mounting operations with a new type fastener has been thoroughly investigated and reviewed by the Suggestion Committee.

Your idea for a new company logo is nothing less than great. Everybody loved your sketch which is already on its way to the engraver.

The information you supplied us about possible future sites for our branch offices is very valuable.

(b) Investigation indicates that it will not be practical to place your idea into effect because it would require tooling that is considerably less efficient than that now in use.

Because of your creativeness and interest our company's image will be enhanced.

I wanted you to know that we are looking into the situation and are analyzing the data you gave us.

(c) If, after one year, you feel that this suggestion is worthy of reconsideration by the Committee, please feel free to resubmit it.

In addition to our sincere thanks, an award of $1,000 will be given to you with your next paycheck.

Your loyalty to the firm, and your contribution to its successful future is very much appreciated. We are not going to forget what you have done for the company.

FORD MOTOR COMPANY

THE AMERICAN ROAD

DEARBORN, MICHIGAN

XXXXXXXXXXXXXX
XXXXXXXXXXXXXX
XXXXXXXXXXXXXX

Dear Paul:

I'm most pleased to inform you that the Management Proposal Committee has authorized me to write this letter of commendation for the adoption of your proposal to fabricate inhouse Part No. 16ZP-738, Details 7 and 34, instead of buying these items from vendors.

Implementation of your suggestion effected direct savings to the Company because of the difference between outside purchase costs and inhouse manufacture costs.

Your inventiveness and initiative are greatly appreciated, and I hope you will continue to submit additional ideas to management when they occur to you.

I'm forwarding a copy of this letter to the Salaried Personnel Section to become a permanent part of your record.

Sincerely,

Thanks for Valuable Suggestion or Information

• OFFER OF SYMPATHY TO EMPLOYEE WHEN OCCASION CALLS FOR IT

If the employee is ill or injured, or if death occurs in the person's immediate family, a personal letter expressing sympathy is appreciated. Moreover, it reinforces a good relationship between employer and employee.

General Rules

Send letter soon after the illness or injury to the employee, or death in the family.

Make it short and to the point.

Write with sincerity and tact.

Don't gush or philosophize.

Alternate Phrases

(a) I was just told this morning about the loss of your father. Please accept my deepest sympathies.

I was very sorry to learn that you are in the hospital. I understand though that it's nothing too serious and that you will be going home soon.

Tom Wilson told me this morning that you had an accident when the two of you were skiing over the weekend. I hope that by the time this reaches you, you will be feeling much better.

(b) Even though your father has been ill for a long time and his passing was not unexpected, I am sure it still hit you pretty hard.

Please accept my best wishes for a speedy recovery. I hope you are back at your desk in the shortest time possible.

Nothing's more uncomfortable than having your leg in a cast, so you have my sympathy. All of us here at the office miss you, and we hope that you will have a speedy recovery.

(c) You are very much in the thoughts of all of us here, and we all send you our sincere condolences.

If there's anything any of us can do for either you or your family, don't hesitate to call.

Best wishes from all of us here to you and your family.

A.G. ROBERTS CO.

700 CRESTVIEW AVENUE

DENNIS, ILLINOIS

XXXXXXXXXXXXXX
XXXXXXXXXXXXX
XXXXXXXXXXXXX

Dear Ross:

We were terribly sorry to hear about the accident that put you into the hospital. We do hope that your injuries are not too serious and that you will be well again real soon.

Your work has been assigned to three of your colleagues who asked me to tell you to please hurry back.

We all wish you a speedy recovery.

Best regards,

**Offer of Sympathy to Employee
When Occasion Calls For It**

• REQUEST FOR REFERENCE FROM PREVIOUS EMPLOYER

The letter and questionnaire used by the Bank of America is similar in form to that used by most companies. Of course, you include only those questions that are applicable to your situation, or you add certain questions that you feel you need to be answered about the applicant.

CONFIDENTIAL INFORMATION

Section I.

1. When did the applicant: a. Enter your employ _____? b. Leave your employ _____?

2. Position(s) occupied _____.

3. Do you regard applicant as: a. Knowledgable _____ b. Industrious _____ c. Innovative _____?

4. Did applicant: a. Follow instructions well _____? b. Cooperate with fellow workers _____?

5. Was applicant satisfactory as to: a. Attendance _____? b. Punctuality _____?

6. Reason for leaving _____

_____

Section II.

1. Do you consider the applicant:

   a. Reliable _____?

   b. Trustworthy _____?

Section III.

Comments _____

_____

BANK OF AMERICA

PERSONNEL RELATIONS

SAN FRANCISCO, CALIFORNIA

XXXXXXXXXXXXXX
XXXXXXXXXXXXXX
XXXXXXXXXXXXXX

Gentlemen:

Application for a position in this bank has been made by Robert J. Anderson from Phoenix, Arizona.

According to Mr. Anderson's resume he was employed by you from January 1979 to January 1982. Moreover, he cited you as a reference.

Your response to our attached questionnaire will be appreciated and held in the strictest confidence. A self-addressed stamped envelope is enclosed for your reply.

Yours truly,

Request for Reference from Previous Employer

• ANSWERING REFERENCE REQUEST

You have to be very careful in writing this letter. Because of the Fair Employment Practices you may not write anything derogatory about any former employee. The best policy is to respond only with facts. Specifically, state the length of time the employee was working at your facility, what his or her title and his/her functions were, and what the reason was for the person's leaving.

General Rules

Stick to facts about your former employee.
Do not give any opinion of the individual, unless it's complimentary.
Be brief and to the point.

Alternate Phrases

(a) Alan Silber came to Abex Company on June 28, 198— as an electronics Engineer, and left us on October 15, 198— as Senior Electronics Engineer.

Josephine Verdin began working for us as an appraiser on March 17, 198—, and held that position until July 1, 198—, when she resigned.

(b) Mr. Silber was a very fine employee who performed well. He has considerable knowledge and ability.

During her stay with us we were satisfied with her performance.

Rubber Stamp

To answer reference inquiries, you can also use a rubber stamp similar to the following:

```
        Applicant was employed by us
        from _____ to _____
        Record _____

        XYZ Company
        Personnel Department
```

JOHN WANAMAKER, PHILADELPHIA

PHILADELPHIA, PENNSYLVANIA

XXXXXXXXXXXXXX
XXXXXXXXXXXXX
XXXXXXXXXXXXX

Dear Ms Gibson:

Evi Anna Smith was employed by John Wanamaker Philadelphia from March 1, 1980 to December 31, 1981.

Her title was Editor, and she worked in the advertising department. In addition to editorial work she did some script writing as well.

Ms Smith's record indicates that she resigned from Wanamaker to accept a position with a New York publishing firm.

Sincerely,

Answering Reference Request

• ENCOURAGING THE EMPLOYEE

Many corporation officials use the letter to inform employees about company activities. The letter is especially effective in reinforcing the sound image your employees have of the company insofar as communicating and caring about the rank and file employees.

General Rules

If you are announcing a specific event, make clear what the event is.
Explain its significance.
Indicate that the employees are an important resource of the company.
Show that you consider the employees' feelings and appreciate their efforts.

Alternate Phrases

(a) We hope you will join in the Holiday Dinner, Wednesday, January 9 in the Employees' Cafeteria from 11:00 a.m. to 5:45 p.m.

As we approach the end of another year, let me thank you for the fine effort you have once again put forth to make this a successful one for our firm.

Our company is so large that it's quite impossible to chat with each of you personally. But a letter can also be personal, and it is my hope that you will feel this one is. I'm quite aware of the important part your work plays in having our company listed in Fortune's 500, and I want to thank you for your efforts.

(b) Music and cash prizes should help to provide a jolly time for all.

To show our appreciation, we are closing our facility next Monday, December 31, so that each of you may have a well-deserved, long weekend during this holiday period.

The outlook for our company's continued success is optimistic. In addition to our minicomputers we are going to put on a strong marketing campaign for our business and personal microcomputers.

(c) We are looking forward to seeing you at this annual festivity.

Again, many thanks for your efforts.

With all the new challenges that lie ahead for our company, we know that you will continue to do your very best to make our products top quality.

JOHN WANAMAKER, PHILADELPHIA

PHILADELPHIA, PENNSYLVANIA

To Our Store Family:

Recently we told you about some expansion plans for John Wanamaker. One of the projects we mentioned was the expansion and inclusion of a budget operation in our Wilmington store.

While the other projects are still in process, we wanted you to know that the Budget Store has been completed and is going to open officially Monday, April 29.

The wing on the old building is beautifully done and we think you will agree with us that the expansion will enhance the store.

Encouraging the Employee

• ANNOUNCING NEW EMPLOYEE BENEFIT PROGRAM

A letter is one of the most effective ways of announcing a new employee benefit program. Thus the employee can study the important announcement at his or her leisure.

General Rules

Describe clearly the important features of the program.
Give the date the program will go into effect.
State how the program will benefit the employee.
If the program is extensive, attach a pamphlet describing all the necessary details.

Alternate Phrases

(a) The Stock Purchase Plan for officers and exempt employees of the Western Computer Corporation is going to be effective March 1, 198—. This plan provides you with a means of acquiring stock in your company on a regular basis and at a below market price.

Two improvements in the Comprehensive Medical Expense Program for active employees will become effective next month, on June 1.

(b) If you become a member of the Plan, in addition to the benefit above, the Company will contribute one half of the stock you purchase. The accompanying booklet will give you further details.

Attached is a copy of an article which will appear in the July 1 Newsletter announcing these improvements.

(c) If after reading the attached booklet you have any questions, please take it up with our Financial Director.

If you have any questions, please let us hear from you.

R. J. REYNOLDS TOBACCO COMPANY

WINSTON-SALEM, NORTH CAROLINA

Dear Fellow Employee:

We are pleased to announce that beginning February 1 the Company will sponsor ten college scholarships for children of both regular employees and former employees who are retired or deceased. The scholarships may be used at any accredited college or university in the United States.

The scholarship recipients will be chosen by the National Merit Scholarship Corporation on the basis of scholastic aptitude, leadership, involvement in school-related activities, and good citizenship as determined by the National Merit Scholarship Corporation. In no instance will any R. J. Reynolds Tobacco Company officer or employee play any part in the selection process of the scholars.

Each scholarship will be a four-year award, covering the undergraduate years. The amount of the scholarship will be determined by the National Merit Scholarship Corporation, and will be based upon the individual winner's financial needs in order to attend the college of his or her choice.

The awards for this year will be announced toward the end of April.

The leaflet describing the scholarship plan is attached. If you have a child who intends to enter college this fall, and who would like to apply for the R. J. Reynolds Tobacco Company scholarship, please request an entry blank from our Scholarship Program Director, in the Personnel Department.

Sincerely,

Announcing New Employee Benefit Program

• LETTER TO EMPLOYEES ABOUT PROFIT-SHARING PLAN

The letter to your employees about profit sharing is an ideal vehicle for an inspirational message. Whether it announces the current value of the units or shares, or talks in general terms of the merit of the plan, this letter offers an opportunity for you to motivate your employees to greater productivity.

General Rules

Keep the tone of the letter light and friendly.

Be generous with your praise for employees' contribution to the value of the profit-sharing plan.

Inspire them to greater effort.

Alternate Phrases

(a) The S.T. Trefor Profit-Sharing Plan had a value of $19.64, as of December 31, 198—. The November 30 value was $20.50. While this was a 4.2% decrease, the $19.64 figure represents an increase of 7% over the value for December 31, 198—, or $18.34.

Here at the Company, our Profit-Sharing Plan, affectionately known as the "spread-the-wealth" plan, has once again provided all of us with an increased unit value. I'm happy to announce that each of our units is now worth $28.47.

I know you are all eagerly awaiting the first evaluation of our recently inaugurated Profit-Sharing Plan. I'm pleased to report that we have had remarkable success so far; each unit is now worth _____.

(b) S.T. Trefor's contribution to the Profit-Sharing Plan for 198— was just under two million dollars. This was the largest company contribution in the history of this plan. The value of the Profit-Sharing Plan is measured, in part, on the success of our company during the year because of the fund's investment in S.T. Trefor stock.

Your company is looking forward to ever-increasing profits, part of which will go into the Profit-Sharing Plan, making the plan more meaningful to you.

As you know, we started the Plan with the hope of contributing toward a better standard of life for all of you. I think you will agree that so far we are heading in the right direction.

(c) Based upon the encouraging level of our business activity so far, I think we have the potential for a really banner year in 198—. This, in turn, will affect the Profit-Sharing Plan beneficially. Thank you all for your cooperation in making this year a successful one.

Thank you for your cooperation We know you will keep up the good work.

With your efforts and a bit of luck, the Company's sales, together with the Profit-Sharing units value, will keep on increasing.

R. J. REYNOLDS TOBACCO COMPANY

WINSTON-SALEM, NORTH CAROLINA

Dear Fellow Employees:

Those of you eligible for Profit Sharing are certainly aware that the fine efforts on the part of every member of the Reynolds team brought a return for last year that should please all of us.

Many of you have expressed your personal pride in being a part of the Company and sharing in this excellent Plan. We, too, are proud of the Plan and feel that the Plan and our Company will always be held in high regard. To ensure this we all have to do our part by being alert to the many ways to improve our places of work, to stop waste, and to increase production. The search for more efficient methods of doing our jobs should never end. The best Profit-Sharing Plan can only be better if those participating in it want it to be so.

Sincerely,

Letter to Employees About Profit-Sharing Plan

• CLARIFYING COMPANY POLICY

When you write to employees to explain or clarify a company policy or action, be sure you keep both objectives in mind. Specifically, make your point clear and present it in a favorable light.

General Rules

State what the policy is that you are referring to.
Explain it simply and succinctly.
Show how the policy will benefit the employee as well as the company.
Include an inspirational message, if the letter lends itself to it.

Alternate Phrases

(a) Last month a new policy was adopted for handling requests from outside persons or companies for permission to reproduce or otherwise use material in our published material.

I believe that Mr. Stevens's talk this morning on our precarious position impressed on each of you the need to do all you can to improve our cash position this quarter.

To ensure that the information we give in answer to requests from customers for costs and shipping dates on our products is accurate, please follow the procedure recommended in this letter.

(b) To simplify the procedure, all you need do is forward the request to Freddie Gorelick, or in his absence, Alan Bing.

In our area, the best and most important way of doing this is for each of us to see that we turn out high-quality work in the shortest possible time. The better the product, the less time that is needed for checking and correcting; and the faster the product is turned out, the less the cost per unit, and the sooner we start to get cash flowing in.

1. Do not give an immediate reply over the phone.
2. Bring the request to your superior.
3. He will check all factors and answer the question.

(c) Please make sure you understand and follow this rule. The proper handling of requests is most important to our public image and, as you know, good image is important to the success of our company.

I know I can count on the cooperation and effort of each of you in this program.

We all benefit from a smoothly run company, so let's do what we can to make our policies work.

(d) & (e) (These paragraphs may be omitted.)

FORD MOTOR COMPANY

THE AMERICAN ROAD

DEARBORN, MICHIGAN

To: The Employees of Ford Motor Company
      Represented by the UAW

When I wrote to you on June 28 at the start of our UAW negotiations, I told you that we would dedicate our full efforts to make free collective bargaining work. In keeping with this pledge, we have today made a proposal to the Union that, in my opinion, should form the basis of a sound and fair settlement of all of the issues in these negotiations.

The offer, to cover a three-year term, contains across-the-board wage increases amounting to an average increase in base rates of seven cents an hour annually, and continuation of the cost-of-living allowance. Further, it contains a new Short Week benefit, improvements in the SUB Plan, and increased retirement benefits. An early edition of your plant newspaper will describe in detail the entire proposal.

Considering the crisis that the American auto industry is going through in trying to compete with the flood of Japanese imports, I know you will appreciate the Company's proposal.

One other thought seems appropriate. This is a "we" organization; and only with the best efforts of ALL of us can we survive these trying times.

I sincerely hope that within the framework of our favorable proposal there will be a prompt and peaceful conclusion to our current negotiations.

Sincerely,

Clarifying Company Policy

- INFORMING EMPLOYEES OF MERGER, AND EXPLAINING
ITS EFFECTS ON PERSONNEL

A merger is usually a complicated procedure, and explaining it to your employees requires a bit more detail than does your usual correspondence. Sometimes a series of letters is necessary to keep employees properly informed of the latest developments. Because a merger inevitably affects personnel, they should be told exactly what the merger means to the company and to them—whether it's good or bad.

General Rules

Make the letter simple and informal.
Give the letter an optimistic tone.
Don't be pedantic in providing details.
Assure the employees of your whole-hearted support.

THE MICROCOMPUTER COMPANY

PHILADELPHIA, PENNSYLVANIA

To Our Employees:

Since April, when I first wrote to you about our proposed merger with Boston Software Company, several important steps have been taken. The first came on May 8 when the stockholders of both companies overwhelmingly approved the plan to merge. Following this, the Interstate Commerce Commission held a public hearing in which it came to a decision to approve the merger.

Consequently, I'm happy to announce that the merger between our company and the Boston Software Company has been finalized, and the name of the new company will be THE BOSTON MICROCOMPUTER COMPANY. The new company will combine the expertise of our hardware engineers with the expertise of their software systems engineers, effecting an outstanding computer system we'll call MICROSOFT for the small business and the home. These are burgeoning fields where success awaits the right kind of computer systems.

We strongly believe that with this merger we have the "right" kind of computer system for this market. As soon as possible, we are going to launch a big, and I might add imaginative, advertising campaign to catch a large share of the business and home computer market.

Insofar as you, our loyal and knowledgable employees are concerned, the merger means more job security than before and promotions as well as increases in salaries as soon as our doubled sales force starts to bring in orders.

Of course, all of this is not going to be in effect overnight, but it's something to look forward to. In the meantime, keep up the good work.

Again, I'm sure you're just as happy as we are that this merger came through so that we can expand our marketing efforts and make "our" MICROSOFT computer system a household word in the business world.

Sincerely,

**Informing Employees of Merger and Explaining
Its Effects on Personnel**

12

How to Improve the Appearance of Your Letters

The impact of a well-written, attractively "packaged" letter is well worth the effort to produce it. Conversely, a skillfully written letter may not do its job properly if you ignore its physical appearance. A letter on a poorly designed letterhead, reproduced on cheap stationery, and typed in an illegible typefont will almost certainly make an unfavorable impression.

The design of the letterhead, the quality of the stationery, the style and neatness and correctness of the typing of a business letter is extremely important. It is the first impression the reader gets of the firm whose name appears at the top of the sheet.

This chapter presents easy-to-follow, precise instructions to give your letter that elegant, yet informal appearance that is used today by successful directors and officers. It also provides helpful hints to structure your letters so that the end product communicates your topic clearly and concisely.

• HOW TO SELECT STATIONERY

Quality paper enhances the effectiveness of a business letterhead. The following features should be considered in selecting paper:

1. Feel
2. Workability
3. Permanence
4. Cost

1. The *feel* of the paper is one of the standards by which letterhead papers are evaluated. High-grade papers have good bulk, crispness, and crackle like a new bank note.
2. The *workability* feature of the paper includes the ease of use, economy of operation, and quality of workmanship the paper provides.
3. The *permanence* feature of the paper is judged by its ability to reproduce clearly defined characters, to withstand erasures, and to permit clear, smooth-flowing signatures.
4. The *cost* feature of the paper is an important factor since it goes into the overhead of the particular office. Management must decide whether the cost justifies the type of letterhead they want to use for business correspondence.

How to Judge the Quality of Paper

Weight. Paper weight is measured by the ream. Each ream consists of 500 sheets, 17″ by 22″. There are 2,000 business letterheads of the 8 1/2″ by 11″ size in a ream. For example, "substance 16" letterhead means 2,000 sheets, letterhead size, weight 16 pounds. The weight of a ream may be 12 pounds, 24 pounds, or even more. The better the quality of paper, the more it weighs.

The 20-pound weight paper is the most commonly used paper for business letters; the 16-pound paper is widely used as general purpose paper within the company. Some executive's letterheads are printed on very fine paper of 24-pound weight.

Content. Paper used for business purposes is made from wood pulp, from cotton fiber, or from a combination of the two. Letterhead paper made from wood pulp is called sulphite bond. It is manufactured in grades 1,2,3, and 4, with grade 1 being the best. The most durable, the best looking, and the most expensive paper is that with a 100 percent cotton content; that is, made entirely from cotton fiber. Formerly, the watermark "rag content" was used by all fine paper mills to describe their better grades of paper containing cotton fibers. The watermark "cotton content" is being used today to describe more adequately the basic fiber contained in fine papers.

Grain. All paper has a "grain," or chief fiber direction. It comes from the process by which the paper is made. In letterhead paper the grain should be parallel to the direction of the writing. (Letterheads to be used with one of the duplicating processes are an exception.) The sheets hug the typewriter platen better and provide a smoother, firmer surface for the impression. Erasing is also easier with the grain parallel to the platen. Every sheet of paper has a "felt" side and a "wire" side. The letterhead should be printed on the felt side.

These criteria for quality paper apply whether your secretary is using a typewriter or a word processor. In other words, even if your secretary is typing your letters into a computer-driven word processor, the letterheads that are put into the printer to print out (via the computer) the letters you dictated should be on quality paper in order to present a good impression of your company.

How to Order Stationery

Even if you get all the specifics over the telephone, ask for a written quotation on cost and on the weight and content of paper, as well as the kind of engraving or printing that will be on it.

In placing the order, specify:

1. the quantity in reams or sheets
2. the weight
3. the content
4. the grain
5. that the letterhead shall be printed on the "felt" side of the paper
6. the size
7. the color
8. the previous order number, if it's a repeat order
9. the supplier's reference number, if it's an initial order
10. that the letterhead shall be identical (or similar) with the attached sample, if that's what you want.

Envelopes for Letterheads

Envelopes of the same quality as the letterhead paper adds to the good impression of the company. However, with today's high cost of quality envelopes, more and more companies choose lesser quality paper for envelopes which are only opened and thrown away by the secretaries. Generally, it's only the letterhead that reaches the addressed executive.

The most popular envelope sizes for business are:

No. 5	4 1/8" by 5 1/4"
No. 6 1/4	3 1/2" by 6"
No. 6 3/4	3 5/8" by 6 1/2"
No. 10	4 1/8" by 9 1/2"

No. 6 3/4" and No. 10 are suitable for 8 1/2" by 11" letterheads. The Monarch size, 3 7/8" by 7 1/2", is used with the smaller executive stationery. No. 5, which is the Baronial size, is also widely used by business executives for their personal stationery.

Continuation Sheets

These sheets, used for second and subsequent pages, should be of the same size and quality as the letterheads. Continuation sheets and letterheads should be ordered together. Comparatively few letters run to more than one page, but the percentage varies with the office. After a secretary has placed two or three orders for stationery, he or she will be able to judge fairly accurately the proportion of continuation sheets to letterheads.

Letterheads for Air Mail

Many companies specify onion-skin paper for lightweight business letterheads used for foreign air mail correspondence. However, letterheads on lightweight paper made from clean, strong cotton fibers are attractive and can withstand frequency of handling.

• THE STRUCTURAL PARTS OF A LETTER

Although today's business letters are rather informal, there are certain conventions your secretary should not ignore. Modern practice still requires the use of certain essential components in business correspondence, as well as one or more optional parts.

essential	*optional*
date line	reference line
inside address	attention line
salutation	subject line
body	identification initials
complimentary close	
signature	

The following section takes each element of a letter, in the order of its position on the page, and explains its proper usage and form.

The Date Line

Every business letter you send out must be dated. An efficient secretary will take care of this automatically, without you dictating the date line. Your only job is to check—when signing the letter—that she is doing it correctly.

Where the date line goes. The standard position of the date line on the page is two to four spaces below the last line of the letterhead, flush with the right-hand margin of the letter. However, the full block and the simplified letter forms, illustrated on pages 266 and 268, should have the date flush with the left-hand margin. If the letter is very short, the date line may be dropped to give a better balance to the page.

With some letterheads, the letter presents a better appearance if the date line is not placed in the standard position. Sometimes the date line is centered on the page, about two spaces below the letterhead. This style should not be used unless the date line is easily distinguished from the letterhead.

How the date line is typed. The typed date line should be in accordance with the following standard procedures:

1. The letter should be dated the day it is dictated, not the day it is typed.
2. The complete date goes on one line.
3. Do not use *nd, st,* or *th* following the day of the month.

4. Do not abbreviate or use figures for the month.

5. Do not spell out the day of the month or the year, except in very formal letters.

right	*wrong*
September 10, 198—	September 10th, 198—
	9/10/8—
	September fifteenth,
	Nineteen hundred and eighty _____

The Reference Line

If a file reference is given in an incoming letter, include a reference line in your reply. Your reference goes beneath the incoming reference. If your letterhead includes a printed reference notation, such as *In reply please refer to,* your reference line comes after it. Otherwise, the reference line comes four spaces beneath the date.

Your Reference # 2032
Our Reference # 4796

The Inside Address

The name, the addressee's title, the name of the company, and the address make up the inside address.

Where to type the inside address. The proper placing of the inside address is important because its position makes an impact on the format of the letter. If the inside address is set too far to the left or right, a corresponding placement of the right-hand margin may make the letter too squat or too thin. If not placed high enough, the inside address may destroy the vertical spacing of the letter and make a second page necessary.

Whether you are using the traditional or indented style, or today's most popular format, the block style, the inside address should not begin less than two spaces, nor more than twelve spaces below the date line, depending upon the length of your letter. The first line of the address should not extend beyond the middle of the page, however.

How the inside address should be typed. There are several rules your secretary should follow in typing inside addresses.

1. The inside address should correspond exactly with the official name of the company you're writing to. If *Company, Co., The,* or *Inc.,* is part of the company's official name, use the form that is in the company title.

2. Do not precede the street number with a word or sign.

right	*wrong*
70 Fifth Avenue	No. 70 Fifth Avenue
70 Fifth Avenue, Room 305	#70 Fifth Avenue
	Room 305, 70 Fifth Avenue

3. There is no set rule about abbreviating words that stand for street direction, such as S. for South and W. for West. But it is a good idea to abbreviate only when there is a good reason, such as to shorten a long line in the inside address.

4. Spell out the numerical names of streets and avenues if they are numbered twelve or under. When figures are used, do not follow with *d, st,* or *th.* Use figures for all house numbers except *One.* Separate the house number from a numerical name of a thoroughfare with a space, a hyphen, and a space. Authorities give different rules for writing addresses, but the following are standard, approved forms.

23 East Twelfth Street	2 Fifth Avenue
23 East 13 Street	234 - 72 Street
One Park Avenue	

5. Never abbreviate the name of a city. States, territories, and possessions of the United States may be abbreviated. The following are the approved forms of abbreviations for states, territories, and possessions:

Alabama ....AL	Kentucky ....KY	Ohio ....OH
Alaska ....AK	Louisiana ....LA	Oklahoma ....OA
Arizona ....AZ	Maine ....ME	Oregon ....OR
Arkansas ....AR	Maryland ....MD	Pennsylvania .....PA
California ....CA	Massachusetts ....MA	Puerto Rico ......PR
Colorado ....CO	Michigan ....MI	Rhode Island .....RI
Connecticut ......CT	Minnesota ....MN	South Carolina ....SC
Delaware ....DE	Mississippi ....MS	South Dakota .....SD
D.C. ....DC	Missouri ....MO	Tennessee ....TN
Florida ....FL	Montana ....MT	Texas ....TX
Georgia ....GA	Nebraska ....NB	Utah ....UT
Guam ....GU	Nevada ....NV	Vermont.........VT
Hawaii ....HI	New Hampshire ......NH	Virginia ....VA
Idaho ....ID	New Jersey ....NJ	Virgin Islands VI
Illinois IL	New Mexico ....NM	Washington .....WA
Indiana ....IN	New York ....NY	West Virginia ....WV
Iowa ....IA	North Carolina ....NC	Wisconsin ....WI
Kansas ....KS	North Dakota ....ND	Wyoming ....WY

Do not abbreviate the following:

Samoa

6. The ZIP Code is the last mandatory item in the address. It follows the city and state address.

7. If there is no street address, put the city and state on separate lines.

8. Do not abbreviate business titles or positions, such as President, Secretary, and Marketing Director. Mr., Ms, Mrs., or Miss precedes the individual's name even when the business title is used.

If a person's business title is short, place it on the first line; if the title is long, coupled with a long name, place the title on the second line.

Mr. James F. Lambert, President
Lambert & Woolf Company

Ms Joan F. Littleton
Advertising Director
Paton & Gibson, Inc.

9. In addressing an individual in a company, corporation or group, place the individual's name on the first line, and the firm's name on the second line.

10. Do not hyphenate a title unless it represents a combination of two offices, such as *Secretary-Treasurer*.

11. When writing to the officer of a corporation who holds several offices, use only the title of the highest office, unless his or her letterhead states it differently.

    Note that the president of a firm normally is considered subordinate to the chairman of the board of directors. All other officers are ranked in their relation to the president. In cases where an executive is both an officer and a member of the board of directors, correspondence should be addressed to him or her in the officer's capacity, unless he/she has indicated otherwise.

12. If a letter is addressed to a particular department in a company, place the name of the company on the first line, and the name of the department on the second line.

The Attention Line

Business letters may be addressed to the company rather than to an individual. However, if you wish to have the letter directed to a particular individual in the firm you may use an "attention line." The advantage of using such a device is that the letter is immediately recognized as a business rather than a personal one and will be opened in the absence of the person to whom it is directed.

Position of the attention line. The attention line should be typed two spaces below the address. The attention line has no punctuation and is not underscored. The attention line may appear in either of the following positions:

Thompson Industries
1800 Plandome Road
Detroit, Michigan

Attention: Mr. Joseph P. Roberts

or

Thompson Industries
1800 Plandome Road
Detroit, Michigan

Attention: Ms Alice J. Varga

It is permissible to direct the letter to the attention of an individual without including his or her given name or initials if you don't know them. (Of course, you can always call up the company and find out the individual's full name from the switchboard operator.)

preferable

Attention: Mr. George H. Richards

permissible

Attention: Mr. Richards

The Salutation

The salutation should be placed two spaces below the inside address, flush with the left-hand margin. If an attention line is used, the salutation should be placed two spaces below the attention line.

The following is the correct way your secretary should type the salutation:

1. Capitalize the first word, the title, and the name.
2. Use a colon following the salutation. A comma is used only in social letters.
3. Mr., Mrs., and Dr., are the only titles that are abbreviated.

Forms of salutation. The form of salutation varies with the tone of the letter and the relationship between the writer and the addressee. See the chart on page 263 for salutations of varying degrees of formality, together with the appropriate complimentary close to use with each.

You may use a personal salutation or complimentary close in your correspondence to close friends. Such salutations as Dear Jim, or Dear Jennifer, are appropriate when you know the recipient very well.

Here are rules that will help you dictate salutations correctly:

1. If the letter is addressed to a man, make the salutation singular; for example, *Dear Mr. Ross,* or *Dear Sir.* If the letter is addressed to a company or group of men, make it plural; for example, *Gentlemen* or *Dear Sirs.*
2. If the letter is addressed to a woman, make the salutation singular; for example, *Dear Ms Ross,* or *Dear Madam.* If the letter is addressed to a company or group of women, make it plural; for example, *Ladies* or *Mesdames.*
3. Never use a designation of any kind after salutation.

right	*wrong*
Dear Mr. Condon:	Dear Mr. Condon, C.P.A.:

4. Never use a business title or designation of position in a salutation.

right	*wrong*
Dear Ms Broder:	Dear Secretary:
	Dear Secretary Broder:

5. Follow a title with the surname:

| *right* | *wrong* |
| Dear Professor Stanton: | Dear Professor: |

6. The proper salutation in a letter that is not addressed to any particular person or firm, such as a general letter of recommendation, is *To Whom It May Concern.* Note that each word begins with a capital.

7. The salutation in a letter addressed to an organization composed of men and women is *Ladies and Gentlemen;* to a man and woman, *Dear Sir and Madam;* to a married couple, *Dear Mr. (or Dr.) and Mrs. Marsh.*

The Subject Line

There is a growing trend in many companies to use a subject line following the salutation. When a subject line is used, it becomes unnecessary to use a lengthy opening sentence to explain the purpose of the letter. Further, the subject line assists the reader in his reference to previous correspondence on the same subject, and also acts as an aid to efficient filing.

How to type the subject line. The subject line should be centered two spaces below the salutation. However, when you use the full block or simplified letter style, the subject line should be flush with the left-hand margin.

Never place the subject line before the salutation. It is part of the body of the letter, not of the heading.

Generally, the subject line is preceded by *Subject,* or *Re.* A colon follows *Subject,* but no punctuation follows *Re.* When the word *Subject* is omitted, the entry should be underscored. If there is more than one line in the subject, underscore the last line only. Be sure to capitalize all the important words in a subject line. The following two examples are the preferred methods for typing subject lines:

June 13, 198—

Martin, Hill, Inc.
Rochester, New York

Gentlemen:

Subject: Child Care Booklet

or

June 13, 198—

Martin, Hill, Inc.
Rochester, New York

Gentlemen:

Re Child Care Booklet

The Body of the Letter

Your secretary will avoid making errors in style by using the following rules as his or her guide:

How to type the body.

1. Single space unless the letter is very short.
2. Double space between paragraphs.
3. When the block style is used, begin each line flush with the left-hand margin of the letter.
4. When the indented or semi-block style is used, indent the first line of each paragraph five to ten spaces.
5. Always indent paragraphs when a letter is double-spaced.

How to write dates within the letter. When the day precedes the month, it is permissible to write the day out, or to use figure. For example, fifth of March, or 5th of March. If the month precedes the day, the figure is always used. For example, March 5.

The importance of consistency in spelling. Some frequently used words in business correspondence, especially as it relates to computer data processing, have two accepted spelling forms, such as *in-house data processing, inhouse DP; stand-alone systems, standalone systems.* If your firm has not adopted a particular standard, the choice is yours. But be consistent! A letter stating in the first paragraph that the Company has decided to do their data processing *in-house,* and two paragraphs later justifying the decision by saying that according to a feasibility study the *inhouse* DP will be more economical, will not leave the reader with a favorable impression.

The Complimentary Close

Where to type the complimentary close. The complimentary close should be typed two spaces below the last line of the letter. It should begin slightly to the right of the center of the page, except in the full block and simplified letter. The complimentary close should never extend beyond the right margin of the letter. In letters of more than one page, at least two lines should be on the page with the close.

How to type the complimentary close.

1. Capitalize only the first word.
2. Follow the complimentary close with a comma. This is a better practice even when open punctuation is used in the inside address.

Forms of complimentary close. The form varies with the tone of the letter and the degree of familiarity between the writer and the addressee. The degree of formality of the complimentary close should correspond with the salutation. The chart on page 263 gives the appropriate complimentary closes for various salutations.

VARIOUS SALUTATIONS AND APPROPRIATE COMPLIMENTARY CLOSES

	Salutations	*Complimentary Closes*
Very Formal	My dear Sir:	Respectfully,
	Sir:	Yours respectfully,
	My dear Madam:	Respectfully,
	Madam:	Yours respectfully,
Formal	Dear Sir:	Very truly yours,
	Dear Madam:	Yours very truly,
	Gentlemen:	Yours truly,
	Ladies:	Very truly yours,
Less Formal	Dear Mr. Suchard:	Sincerely,
	Dear Ms Sheean:	Sincerely yours,
	Dear Dr. Lubow:	Yours sincerely,

(Most business correspondences use these forms rather than the formal forms.)

Personal	Dear Mr. Suchard:	Yours cordially,
	Dear Ms Sheean:	Cordially,
	Dear Dr. Lubow:	Cordially yours,

(Implying personal acquaintance or previous friendly correspondence.)

Do not confuse *respectfully* with *respectively*. The latter means with respect to each of two or more, in the order named.

The Signature

What to include in the signature. Your signature on a business letter usually consists of your written signature, your typed name and business title, and the name of your division or department, if appropriate. Your typed name can be omitted if it appears on the letterhead.

The inclusion in the signature of your business title or position indicates that you are writing the letter in your official capacity. Thus, if you write a letter on the firm's stationery about a purely personal matter, your position is not included in the signature.

Firms of attorneys, certified public accountants and the like frequently sign letters manually with the firm's name, particularly if the letter expresses a professional opinion or gives professional advice.

Where to place the signature. The firm's name should be typed two spaces below the complimentary close; the writer's name four spaces below the firm's name; and the writer's position either on the same line or on the next line. When the firm name is not included, the writer's name and position should go four spaces below the complimentary close.

When the inside address is typed in block form, the signature should be aligned with the first letter of the complimentary close. When the indented form is used in the inside address, the signature is aligned with the third or fourth letters of the complimentary close. In either case, the lines of the signature should be blocked, unless an unusually long line makes this arrangement impractical.

No line of the signature should extend beyond the right-hand margin of the letter.

How the signature should be typed.

1. The signature should appear exactly as you sign your name.

right   *wrong*

Helen P. Dunnel	*Helen P. Dunnel*
Helen P. Dunnel President	H.P. Dunnel President

2. Business titles and degree letters follow the typed signature. No title precedes either the written or typed signature.

The secretary's signature. When your secretary signs your name to a letter, his or her initials should be placed immediately below it.

Yours truly,

Lyle R. Deen

Lyle R. Deen *M.B.*
Treasurer

When the secretary signs a letter in his/her own name, your name, official title, and division or department should be typed below his or hers.

right   *wrong*

Secretary to Charles P. Doyle Marketing Director Electronics Division	Secretary to C.P. Doyle Electronics Division

Identification Initials

The identification line shows who dictated the letter and who typed it. The only purpose of the identification line is for reference by the business organization writing the letter.

If your company requires the usual identification line, the initials of the dictator and the secretary should be placed flush with the left-hand margin, two spaces below the last line of the signature. Capitals are usually used for the dictator's initials, and lower case letters are usually used for the typist's initials.

The following are the various accepted forms for typing initials:

HD/ca   HD:ca   HDca

• LETTER STYLE

A competent secretary or stenographer gives careful attention to the mechanical setup of the letter—the arrangement on the page, the width of the margins, and the position of the date, the inside address, the salutation, and the complimentary close. Modern business practice has established certain conventions, and observance of these conventions reflects an efficient office.

The Format

Selecting an appropriate format for your business letters is good business policy, since it adds to the overall impression of you and your company. Therefore, make sure that your secretary uses the best format for your purpose.

Style of type. When your secretary is planning the layout of a letter, he/she must know the approximate number of words that will fit comfortably on a page. This is partly determined by the kind of type on the machine he/she uses.

The most popular forms of type (whether the secretary uses word-processing or electric typewriter) are called "pica" and "elite." (There are other types of styles that you can order, if you wish.) Pica type produces ten characters per inch across a page, or 85 characters across a sheet of standard size letter paper, 8 1/2 by 11 inches.

The elite style of type is smaller than the pica, and permits twelve characters per inch across a page, or 102 characters across an 8 1/2 by 11 inch sheet.

Margins. A letter can't present a balanced, attractive appearance unless the typist selects the right margin width for the length of the letter. An experienced typist can do this by just glancing at her steno book. Suppose, for example, that a particular letter contains 200 words. The address for a letter of this length should begin about three inches from the top of the page. The proper place for the complimentary close and signature would be about three and a half inches from the bottom of the 8 1/2 by 11 inch sheet.

The margins should be set up so that the top and bottom and both sides form a balanced arrangement. In general, the shorter the letter, the wider the margin it needs.

Spacing. Single-spaced letter with double spacing between paragraphs is the form most widely used in business correspondence.

PRENTICE-HALL, INC.

ENGLEWOOD CLIFFS, N.J. 07632

Telex No. 13-5423

July 16, 198—

Ms Sheila Jones
The Modern School for Secretaries
12 Harrington Place
Greenpoint, N.Y.

Dear Ms Jones:

In reply to your request for examples of current business letter styles, this letter is an example of the block style letter which is the standard at Prentice-Hall. We have reproduced it in our Employee Manual so that everyone is familiar with the form and the instructions for its use.

Since Prentice-Hall is a leading exponent of modern business methods, they naturally use the most efficient letter form. This style saves time and energy.

As you see, there are no indentations. Everything, including the date and the complimentary close, begins at the extreme left.

Our dictaphone typists always use this form, unless the dictator instructs otherwise.

Sincerely,

Martha Scott
Correspondence Chief

MS:cf

(The distinguishing feature of the Block Style of letter is that all the structural parts of the letter begin flush with the left margin. There are no indentations. Also, open punctuation is used in the address and signature.)

PRENTICE-HALL, INC.

ENGLEWOOD CLIFFS, N.J. 07632

Telex No. 13-5423

July 16, 198—

Your reference 12:-3:1

Ms Sheila Jones
The Modern School for Secretaries
12 Harrington Place
Greenpoint, N.Y.

Dear Ms Jones:

You asked me if there is any one style of setting up a letter that is used more than the others. Probably more business concerns use the block style of letter than any other style, because its marginal uniformity saves time for the typist. This letter is an example of the block style.

As you can see, the inside address is blocked and the paragraph beginnings are aligned with the left margin. Open punctuation is used in the address.

The date and reference lines are flush with the right margin. The date line is two spaces below the letterhead, and the reference line is two spaces below the date line. The complimentary close begins slightly to the right of the center of the page. Both lines of the signature are aligned with the complimentary close.

As the dictator's name is typed in the signature, it is not considered necessary to include his or her initials in the identification line.

Sincerely yours,

Martha Scott
Correspondence Chief
Accounting
Department

cf

(The distinguishing feature of this letter is that it contains a reference line, and that the inside address and paragraphs are blocked, flush with the left-hand margin. Open punctuation is used in the address and signature, and the dictator's initials are not included in the identification line.)

PRENTICE-HALL, INC.

ENGLEWOOD CLIFFS, N.J. 07632

Telex No. 13-5423

July 16, 198—

Ms Sheila Jones
The Modern School for Secretaries
12 Harrington Place
Greenpoint, New York

Dear Ms Jones:

Subject: Business Letter Styles

Most companies have a definite preference as to letter style. Many leading business corporations insist that all letters be typed in semi-block style. This style combines an attractive appearance with utility. Private secretaries, who are not usually concerned with mass production of correspondence, favor it.

This style differs from the block form in that the first line of each paragraph is indented five or ten spaces. As in all letters, there is a double space between paragraphs.

The date line is flush with the left margin, two or four spaces below the letterhead. The complimentary close begins slightly to the left of the center of the page. All lines of the signature are aligned with the complimentary close.

Very sincerely yours,

Martha Scott
Correspondence Chief

MS/cf

(The distinguishing feature of a Semi Block Style of letter is that all structural parts of the letter begin flush with the left-hand margin, but the first line of each paragraph is indented five or ten spaces. Open punctuation is used in the address and signature, and a subject line is included.)

PRENTICE-HALL, INC.

ENGLEWOOD CLIFFS, N.J. 07632

Telex No. 13-5423

July 16, 198—

Ms Sheila Jones,
    The Modern School for Secretaries,
        12 Harrington Place,
            Greenpoint, New York

Dear Ms Jones:

This is an example of the indented style of letter which many conservative organizations still use. The indented style is correct, however, for any type of firm.

Each line of the address is indented five spaces more than the preceding line. The beginning of each paragraph is indented the same as the third line of the address, which is ten spaces. The complimentary close begins a few spaces to the right of the center of the page, and the lines of the signature are aligned with the complimentary close. Closed punctuation is used in the address but not in the signature.

Very truly yours,

Martha Scott
Correspondence Chief

Ms:cf
Enc.

(The distinguishing feature of the Indented Style of letter is that each line of address is indented five spaces more than the preceding line. The first line of each paragraph is indented ten spaces. Close punctuation is used in the address but not in the signature.)

PRENTICE-HALL, INC.

ENGLEWOOD CLIFFS, N.J. 07632

Telex No. 13-5423

July 16, 198—

Dear Ms Jones:

Every correspondence manual should include a sample of the official style. It is used by executives and professional individuals when writing personal letters, and it looks very well on the executive-size letterhead.

The structural parts of the letter differ from the standard arrangement only in the position of the inside address. The salutation is placed two to five spaces below the date line, depending upon the length of the letter. It establishes the left margin of the letter. The inside address is written in block form, flush with the left margin, from two to five spaces below the final line of the signature. Open punctuation is used in the address.

The identification line, if used, is placed two spaces below the last line of the address.

Sincerely yours,

Martha Scott
Correspondence Chief

Ms Sheila Jones
The Modern School for Secretaries
12 Harrington Place
Greenpoint, New York

MS/cf

(The distinguishing feature of the Official Style of letter is that the inside address is placed below the signature, flush with the left-hand margin, instead of before the salutation. The identification line and enclosure notations, if any, are typed two spaces below the last line of the address. Open punctuation is used.)

PRENTICE-HALL, INC.

ENGLEWOOD CLIFFS, N.J. 07632

Telex No. 13-5423

July 16, 198—

Ms Sheila Jones
The Modern School for Secretaries
12 Harrington Place
Greenpoint, New York

Dear Ms Jones:

This is an example of a short letter. The style differs from the previous sample letters in that the lines are double-spaced, and the beginning of each paragraph is indented five or ten spaces.

As you can see, the date is typed in the conventional position, and the complimentary close and the signature below it start a few spaces to the right of the center of the page.

Very truly yours,

Martha Scott
Correspondence Chief

MS:cf

(The distinguishing feature of a short letter is that though the body of the letter is double-spaced for better appearance, the inside address, which uses open punctuation, is still single-spaced. Each paragraph is indented five or ten spaces to indicate a new paragraph.)

Common sense can be your best guide in determining how a letter should be spaced. If a letter contains so few words that a single-spaced treatment would seem to make the words stand lonesome on a page, double-spacing would be called for (or the use of smaller stationery). Generally, letters of 100 words or less look best double-spaced.

The format should be pleasing to the eye. When it comes to deciding how the various parts of a business letter should be arranged on a page, there is no one style that might be considered "the best." The choice of form to be used is usually a matter of preference. Many business concerns and executives have standards for letter styles. On pages 266 through 271 are examples of the more popular formats that can be used as a guide in determining which best suits your purpose and taste.

Indention or tabulation. Indention is a device that creates a "frame within a frame." It is especially effective when the letter is typed in the block form. Because the left hand margin of the block letter is so strictly established, the indention of certain material stands out particularly well—in the same way that a "mat" serves to set off a picture within its initial frame.

example

The envelope we're enclosing is to make it easy for you to turn this sheet over and write us—

       to have our representative call,
       to send you our price list,
       or, to say just what you think of us.

We hope it's good, but if it isn't. . . . .

Numbering. Numbering is used effectively to set off various points that are later detailed. The numbered items may be listed one beneath the other, or they may be run together within a paragraph. If the latter method is used, the numbers should be enclosed in parentheses, e.g., (1). If the listing method is used, the following procedure is advised.

1. Indent five spaces from each margin of the letter—more if necessary to center the material.

2. Precede each item with a number, followed by a period, e.g.,

                4. Quality Control

3. Begin each line of the indented material two spaces to the right of the number.

4. Single space the material within each item, but double space between items, e.g.,

                4. Quality Control—in
                   Manufacturing

> Packaging
> Shipping
>
> 5. Security—in
>   Physical Access to the plant
>   Authorized personnel to the
>   design room

Sometimes the typist will want to use both the listing and the run-in methods in a single letter, especially when the subject matter requires subdivision within the original numbering of facts.

Underscoring and capitalization. A line under an important phrase or topical heading is used for emphasis in presenting facts. Another device for attracting the reader's attention is the capitalization of a phrase or heading. But whether they are used individually or together, both are seasonings that must be used with caution. Too much underscoring and capitalization makes the reader feel that much ado is being made about nothing. It distracts his or her attention, rather than captures it.

Forms of punctuation. The punctuation of the heading, inside address, and signature may be either open or close, as the previous sample letters displayed. But whichever style is selected for one part of the letter, must be used for all three. Again, consistency of style can make or break the appearance of a letter. Hence, the punctuation of the heading sets the style for the rest of the letter.

1. *Open punctuation* means the omission of all commas and periods at the ends of lines in the heading, the inside address, and the signature.

2. *Close (or closed) punctuation,* no longer popular, requires that punctuation be used after each line in the heading, the inside address, and the signature—if the typed name of the letter writer is followed by his or her official title.

Here's an example of each of the two styles of punctuation:

open

June 19, 198—

Mr. William J. Johnson
97 Arden Street
Philadelphia, PA

Dear Mr. Johnson:

> Sincerely,
> (signature)
> Nancy Jorgensen
> Vice-President

close

June 19, 198—

Mr. William J. Johnson,
97 Arden Street,
Philadelphia, PA.

Dear Mr. Johnson:

                                           Sincerely,
                                           (signature)
                                           Nancy Jorgensen,
                                           Vice-President

It's important to remember that the salutation is usually followed by a colon, and the complimentary close by a comma, no matter which of the two punctuation forms is used for the other parts of the letter.

Appendix **A**

Letter Master Checklist: Essentials for the Successful Letter

To make this section as useful as possible for the busy executive whose many responsibilities include writing all types of letters, it is organized as a reference guide in alphabetical order.

1. ADDRESS FORM

For the overall impression of a letter it is quite important that the address form is proper. For formal letters, the charts in Appendix B provide the correct titles of U.S. and foreign officials. Proper address form for less formal letters, however, is just as important. This is especially true when the letter goes to a woman executive. When the letter goes to a man executive, the address form is rather simple. For example,

> Mr. Robert Reed
> Vice-President, Marketing
> Brady Corporation
> Waverly Place
> Houston, Texas

But, when the letter goes to a woman executive, the title can be "Miss," "Mrs." or "Ms" (which, by the way, is *not* an abbreviation, and consequently does not require a period after it just as "Miss" does not). To play it safe, more and more executives use the "Ms," which is an appropriate form of address to either a single or a married woman. For example,

Ms Jennifer Reed
Vice-President, Marketing
Brady Corporation
Waverly Place
Houston, Texas.

The latest trend in the business world is to go one step further and leave out the title in the address form entirely. For example,

Robert Reed
Vice-President, Marketing

and

Jennifer Reed
Vice-President, Marketing.

2. COMPLIMENTARY CLOSE

The complimentary close, which is typed two spaces below the last paragraph of the letter, should correspond with the salutation both in form and the degree of formality. In other words, if you began your letter with the very formal "My dear Sir:" or "Ladies:" you wouldn't use "Cordially yours," as a complimentary close. Similarly, if your salutation reads "Dear Henry:" you wouldn't use the complimentary close "Respectfully yours."

3. FIRST SENTENCE, FIRST PARAGRAPH

With your first sentence, first paragraph you should indicate not only the subject of your letter but establish its mood as well.

Your opening sentence can be complimentary, gracious, provocative, challenging, or a statement of facts—depending on the subject of your letter and the impact you wish to have on the addressee. The main thing to remember is that it is your first sentence that prepares the reader for the rest of your communication. Here, for example, is the first sentence of a "General Sales Letter" that is bound to attract the reader's attention, if he or she is thinking of a vacation trip.

"If you are planning to take a vacation trip this year, we have a suggestion which can make this the best trip you ever made—and can save you money too."

For another example, here's a rather provocative opening of a "Follow-Through Sales Letter:"

"The bird is the fastest moving living creature. Speeds higher than 185 mph have been attributed to peregrine falcons. Homo sapiens, of course, move less quickly. But there is one group which is known for its remarkable mobility—the business executive."

Through the courtesy of Fortune © *1979 Time Inc.*

For still another example, here's the first sentence, first paragraph of a letter that intends to relay harsh realities to the reader.

"The premium of 2% cash discount is for early payment. Since we did not receive your check for our invoice #12576 until 30 days after the discount period expired, we cannot allow your deduction."

And finally, here's an example of the beginning of a letter that combines criticism with graciousness.

"In a recent commentary 'Disciplining Teachers,' your associate editor observed that criticizing schools and complaining about teachers seems to be "increasingly fashionable." He is uncomfortably correct. But, may I also say, that it's a myth that our schools are failing."

4. FORMAT

The primary consideration in deciding upon a format is that it should be pleasing to the eye. Actually, when it comes to determining how the various parts of a business letter should be arranged on a page, there is no one style that might be considered "the best." The choice of form to be used is usually a matter of preference. A letter can be in a block form or indented (the first line of each paragraph indented five or ten spaces), but as long as there's a nice wide margin all around the single-spaced letter, it will give a balanced, attractive appearance. If the letter is quite short, it will look better if it is double-spaced. Moreover, a double-spaced letter should use the indented form to indicate new paragraphs. (For a detailed discussion on format see Chapter 12.)

5. LAST SENTENCE

The last sentence should reinforce the first sentence and the topic of the letter. It should not jar the reader. Thus, for example, if it's a letter politely reminding the customer of an outstanding bill, the last sentence cannot suddenly be a sharp one. Conversely, if the letter is a firm, no-nonsense rejection of an offer or an applicant, the last sentence should not be, abruptly, a really warm one. In short, the last sentence should be in tune with the rest of the letter and leave the reader with a clear understanding of the subject and the intent of the letter. For example, here's the last sentence of a letter written to a vacation-bound person.

"It would be our pleasure to help you make this the most interesting, relaxed, and economical trip you ever had."

For another example, here's the last paragraph of a letter for "Contacting Inactive Account:"

"Won't you please let me know personally why you have stopped placing orders with us? I would greatly appreciate it."

As a final example, here's the last sentence of a letter for "Demanding Retraction:"

"We are looking forward to the retraction of the above item as soon as possible in your newspaper."

6. LETTERHEAD

Quality paper enhances the effectiveness of a business letterhead. But the best quality paper won't help if the printed letterhead is offensively ostentatious. The most impressive business letterheads are simple and subdued. For example, a simple brown letterhead printed on ivory or light tan quality paper gives the impression of a company that knows its own worth and doesn't need to shout it from the roof-tops. That doesn't mean, however, that a bold, black letterhead printed on white paper cannot be just as tasteful and impressive. The fact is that the choice of printed letterhead is entirely a matter of taste and preference. The main thing is that it reflects the personality of the company and the particular field in which the company is operating.

7. PAPER

Quality paper can be judged by its bulk, by its ability to reproduce the typewritten material clearly, and by the way it can withstand erasures. The most commonly used paper for business letters is the 20-pound weight paper, because it satisfies all the above criteria. (For an in-depth discussion on paper, see Chapter 12.)

8. PARAGRAPHS

To make your letters interesting, you should vary the length of your paragraphs. In fact, a one-sentence or even a one-word paragraph can sparkle the interest of the most indifferent addressee. Of course, an explanatory paragraph enlarging upon the eye-catching exclamation should follow. For example, here are the first two paragraphs from a letter written to a "nonactive" client account.

"Tell us what you think!

As a valued client, we'd like your opinion as to how we could improve our services."

For another example, here are the first two paragraphs from a letter written by an airline company.

"Our apologies!

I sincerely regret that we were unable to operate your August 3 flight on time, and apologize for the inconvenience it caused you."

For still another example, here are the first two paragraphs from a letter soliciting for charitable contribution.

"Help!

We really need your help. The work load of Hope Indian School has tripled in the past year due to increased enrollment. As a result, so much more is asked of us."

9. SALUTATION

The form of salutation depends on the relationship between you and the addressee as well as the tone of the letter. If it's a formal business letter addressed to a man, make the salutation singular; for example, "Dear Mr. Silvers," or "Dear Sir," if you want to be really formal. If the letter is addressed to a company or group of men, make it plural; for example, "Gentlemen," or "Dear Sirs."

If the formal business letter is addressed to a woman, make the salutation singular; for example, "Dear Ms Silvers," or "Dear Madam," if you want to be really formal. If the letter is addressed to a company or group of women, make it plural; for example, "Ladies," or "Mesdames."

Of course, if you know the addressee very well, even if it's a business letter, it's appropriate to make the salutation "Dear Jim," or "Dear Jennifer." (For a thorough discussion on salutation, see Chaper 12.)

10. SIGNATURE

Your signature on a business letter usually consists of your written signature above your typed name and business title, and the name of your division or department, if appropriate. Business titles and degree letters follow the typed signature. For example, *Paul Steward, President, Patricia Wolner, Ph.D.,* or *James Fall, Director.* No title (*Mr.* or *Ms* or *Dr.* or *Professor*) precedes either the written or the typed signature.

11. STYLE

The style of your letter and the style of your writing should be more than just gracious and correct, it should reflect your personality. Consequently, whether it's a formal or informal letter that you are writing or dictating, don't use stiff, pale words. Try to inject colorful, active verbs that will let your personality shine through, and that will make reading your letters a pleasure.

12. TONE

Just as the tone of your voice will reflect the mood you're in, the tone of your letter will mirror your attitude and your thoughts. Consequently, if you have a condescending attitude toward the person you're writing to, the tone of your letter will reflect that, no matter how hard you're trying to hide it behind "nice" words. Similarly, artificial geniality or warmth is easily detected in a letter, regardless of how careful the writer was in composing the letter. Therefore, the best way to insure that the tone of your letter doesn't strike some "sour notes" is for you to be sincere. The tone of a letter written with sincerity will always be well received.

Appendix B

Proper Address Forms

$\mathbf{P}$roper address form is an essential part of your letter. Consequently, just as you would not tolerate a letter leaving your office with poor grammar, misspelled words, or sloppy erasures, you should not condone a casual approach to forms of address. The reason is a very practical one: should you offend your reader by addressing him or her incorrectly, you might completely nullify the effect of an otherwise perfect letter. It is an extraordinary person who does not take his or her title seriously, regardless of rank.

The following charts will save you substantial time and effort when you write to a person with an official title. The charts have been compiled into the following categories:

> United States Government Officials
> State and Local Government Officials
> Court Officials
> United States Diplomatic Representatives
> Foreign Officials and Representatives
> The Armed Forces Church Dignitaries
> College and University Officials
> The United Nations
> The Organization of American States
> The British Peerage, Baronets, and Knights
> British Government Officials

Each chart gives you the correct forms of written address, salutation, and complimentary close to be used in letters to titled persons. This handy reference guide will serve you well on these important occasions.

UNITED STATES GOVERNMENT OFFICIALS

Personage	Envelope and Inside Address	Formal Salutation	Informal Salutation	Formal Close	Informal Close
The President	The President The White House Washington, D. C.	Mr. President:	Dear Mr. President:	Respectfully yours,	Very respectfully yours,
Former President of the United States[1]	The Honorable William R. Blank (local address)	Sir:	Dear Mr. Blank:	Respectfully yours,	Very truly yours, *or* Sincerely yours,
The Vice President of the United States	The Vice President of the United States United States Senate Washington 25, D. C.	Sir:	Dear Mr. Vice President:	Respectfully,	Very truly yours, *or* Sincerely yours,
The Chief Justice of the United States Supreme Court	The Chief Justice of the United States The Supreme Court of the United States Washington 25, D. C.	Sir:	Dear Mr. Chief Justice:	Respectfully,	Very truly yours, *or* Sincerely yours,
Associate Justice of the United States Supreme Court	Mr. Justice Blank The Supreme Court of the United States Washington 25, D. C.	Sir: *or* Mr. Justice:	Dear Mr. Justice:	Very truly yours,	Sincerely yours,
Retired Justice of the United States Supreme Court	The Honorable William R. Blank (local address)	Sir:	Dear Justice Blank:	Very truly yours,	Sincerely yours,
The Speaker of the House of Representatives	The Honorable the Speaker of the House of Representatives Washington 25, D. C. *or* The Honorable William R. Blank Speaker of the House of Representatives Washington 25, D. C.	Sir:	Dear Mr. Speaker: *or* Dear Mr. Blank:	Very truly yours,	Sincerely yours,
Former Speaker of the House of Representatives	The Honorable William R. Blank (local address)	Sir:	Dear Mr. Blank:	Very truly yours,	Sincerely yours,
Cabinet Officers addressed as "Secretary"[2] *(man)*	The Honorable the Secretary of State Washington 25, D. C. (formal) The Honorable William R. Blank Secretary of State Washington 25, D. C. (informal) The Honorable William R. Blank Secretary of State of the United States of America Washington 25, D. C. (if written from abroad)	Sir:	Dear Mr. Secretary:	Very truly yours,	Sincerely yours,

[1] If a former president has a title, address him by it. For example, General of the Army Dwight D. Eisenhower.

[2] Titles for cabinet secretaries are Secretary of State; Secretary of the Treasury; Secretary of Defense; Secretary of the Interior; Secretary of Agriculture; Secretary of Commerce; Secretary of Labor; and Secretary of Health, Education, and Welfare.

UNITED STATES GOVERNMENT OFFICIALS *continued*

Personage	Envelope and Inside Address	Formal Salutation	Informal Salutation	Formal Close	Informal Close
Cabinet Officer (woman)[3]	Same as for a man	Madam:	Dear Madam Secretary:	Very truly yours,	Sincerely yours,
Postmaster General	The Honorable William R. Blank The Postmaster General Washington 25, D. C.	Sir:	Dear Mr. Postmaster General:	Very truly yours,	Sincerely yours,
The Attorney General	The Honorable William R. Blank The Attorney General Washington 25, D. C.	Sir:	Dear Mr. Attorney General:	Very truly yours,	Sincerely yours,
Former Cabinet Officer	The Honorable William R. Blank (local address)	Dear Sir:	Dear Mr. Blank:	Very truly yours,	Sincerely yours,
Under Secretary of a Department	The Honorable William R. Blank Under Secretary of Labor Washington 25, D. C.	Dear Mr. Blank:	Dear Mr. Blank:	Very truly yours,	Sincerely yours,
United States Senator (man)	The Honorable William R. Blank United States Senate Washington 25, D. C.	Dear Senator Blank:	Dear Senator Blank:	Very truly yours,	Sincerely yours,
United States Senator (woman)[3]	The Honorable Louise I. Blank United States Senate Washington 25, D. C.	Dear Senator Blank:	Dear Senator Blank: *or* Dear Mrs. (Miss) Blank:	Very truly yours,	Sincerely yours,
Former Senator	The Honorable William R. Blank (local address)	Dear Senator Blank: *or* Dear Sir:	Dear Senator Blank:	Very truly yours,	Sincerely yours,
Senator—elect	Honorable William R. Blank Senator—elect United States Senate Washington 25, D. C.	Dear Mr. Blank *or* Dear Sir:	Dear Mr. Blank:	Very truly yours,	Sincerely yours,
Committee Chairman— United States Senate	The Honorable William R. Blank, Chairman Committee on Foreign Affairs United States Senate Washington 25, D. C.	Dear Mr. Chairman:	Dear Mr. Chairman: *or* Dear Senator Blank:	Very truly yours,	Sincerely yours,

[3]In addressing a woman official and her husband, the customary form of addressing a husband and his wife applies.

UNITED STATES GOVERNMENT OFFICIALS *continued*

Personage	Envelope and Inside Address	Formal Salutation	Informal Salutation	Formal Close	Informal Close
Subcommittee Chairman— United States Senate	The Honorable William R. Blank, Chairman, Subcommittee on Foreign Affairs United States Senate Washington 25, D. C.	Dear Senator Blank:	Dear Senator Blank:	Very truly yours,	Sincerely yours,
United States Representative (man)	The Honorable William R. Blank House of Representatives Washington 25, D. C. (Washington, D. C. Office) The Honorable William R. Blank Representative in Congress (local address) (when away from Washington, D. C.)	Dear Sir:	Dear Mr. Blank:	Very truly yours,	Sincerely yours,
United States Representative (woman)	The Honorable Louise Blank[3] House of Representatives Washington 25, D. C.	Dear Madam: *or* Dear Representative Blank:	Dear Mrs. (Miss) Blank:	Very truly yours,	Sincerely yours,
Representative at Large	The Honorable William R. Blank House of Representatives Washington 25, D. C.	Dear Sir: *or* Dear Mr. Blank:	Dear Mr. Blank:	Very truly yours,	Sincerely yours,
Former Representative	The Honorable William R. Blank (local address)	Dear Sir: *or* Dear Mr. Blank:	Dear Mr. Blank:	Very truly yours,	Sincerely yours,
Territorial Delegate	The Honorable William R. Blank Delegate of Puerto Rico House of Representatives Washington 25, D. C.	Dear Sir: *or* Dear Mr. Blank:	Dear Mr. Blank:	Very truly yours,	Sincerely yours,
Resident Commissioner	The Honorable William R. Blank Resident Commissioner of (Territory) House of Representatives Washington 25, D. C.	Dear Sir: *or* Dear Mr. Blank:	Dear Mr. Blank:	Very truly yours,	Sincerely yours,
Directors or Heads of Independent Federal Offices, Agencies, Commissions, Organizations, etc.	The Honorable William R. Blank Director, Mutual Security Agency Washington 25, D. C.	Dear Mr. Director (Commissioner, etc.):	Dear Mr. Blank:	Very truly yours,	Sincerely yours,
Librarian of Congress	The Honorable William R. Blank Librarian of Congress Washington 25, D. C.	Dear Sir: *or* Dear Mr. Blank:	Dear Mr. Blank:	Very truly yours,	Sincerely yours,

[3]In addressing a woman official and her husband, the customary form of addressing a husband and his wife applies.

Personage	Envelope and Inside Address	Formal Salutation	Informal Salutation	Formal Close	Informal Close
Other High Officials of the United States, in general: Public Printer, Comptroller General	The Honorable William R. Blank Public Printer Washington 25, D.C. The Honorable William R. Blank Comptroller General of the United States Washington 25, D. C.	Dear Sir: *or* Dear Mr. Blank:	Dear Mr. Blank:	Very truly yours,	Sincerely yours,
Secretary to the President	The Honorable William R. Blank Secretary to the President The White House Washington 25, D. C.	Dear Sir: *or* Dear Mr. Blank:	Dear Mr. Blank:	Very truly yours,	Sincerely yours,
Secretary to the President with military rank	Major General William R. Blank Secretary to the President The White House Washington 25, D. C.	Dear Sir: *or* Dear General Blank:	Dear General Blank:	Very truly yours,	Sincerely yours,
Assistant Secretary to the President	The Honorable William R. Blank Assistant Secretary to the President The White House Washington 25, D. C.	Dear Sir: *or* Dear Mr. Blank:	Dear Mr. Blank:	Very truly yours,	Sincerely yours,
Press Secretary to the President	Mr. William R. Blank Press Secretary to the President The White House Washington 25, D. C.	Dear Sir: *or* Dear Mr. Blank:	Dear Mr. Blank:	Very truly yours,	Sincerely yours,

STATE AND LOCAL GOVERNMENT OFFICIALS

Personage	Envelope and Inside Address	Formal Salutation	Informal Salutation	Formal Close	Informal Close
Governor of a State or Territory[1]	*Formal* The Honorable the Governor of New York Albany, New York *Informal* The Honorable William (or Nancy) R. Blank Governor of New York Albany, New York	Sir: *or* Madam:	Dear Governor Blank:	Respectfully yours,	Very sincerely yours,
Acting Governor of a State or Territory	The Honorable William (or Nancy) R. Blank Acting Governor of Connecticut Hartford, Connecticut	Sir: *or* Madam:	Dear Mr. Blank: *or* Dear Ms Blank:	Respectfully yours,	Very truly yours,

[1]The form of addressing Governors varies in the different states. The form given here is the one used in most states. In Massachusetts by law and in some other states by courtesy, the form is *His Excellency, the Governor of Massachusetts.*

Personage	Envelope and Inside Address	Formal Salutation	Informal Salutation	Formal Close	Informal Close
Lieutenant Governor	**Formal** The Honorable the Lieutenant Governor of Iowa Des Moines, Iowa *Informal* The Honorable William R. Blank Lieutenant Governor of Iowa Des Moines, Iowa	Sir:	Dear Mr. Blank:	Respectfully yours, *or* Very truly yours,	Sincerely yours,
Secretary of State	**Formal** The Honorable the Secretary of State of New York Albany, New York *Informal* The Honorable William R. Blank Secretary of State of New York Albany, New York	Sir:	Dear Mr. Secretary:	Very truly yours,	Sincerely yours,
Attorney General	The Honorable William R. Blank Attorney General of Massachusetts Boston, Massachusetts	Sir:	Dear Mr. Attorney General:	Very truly yours,	Sincerely yours,
President of the Senate of a State	The Honorable William R. Blank President of the Senate of the State of Virginia Richmond, Virginia	Sir:	Dear Mr. Blank:	Very truly yours,	Sincerely yours,
Speaker of the Assembly of The House of Representatives[2]	The Honorable William R. Blank Speaker of the Assembly of the State of New York Albany, New York	Sir:	Dear Mr. Blank:	Very truly yours,	Sincerely yours,
Treasurer, Auditor, or Comptroller of a State	The Honorable William R. Blank Treasurer of the State of Tennessee Nashville, Tennessee	Dear Sir:	Dear Mr. Blank:	Very truly yours,	Sincerely yours,
State Senator	The Honorable William R. Blank The State Senate Trenton, New Jersey	Dear Sir: *or* Dear Madam:	Dear Senator Blank:	Very truly yours,	Sincerely yours,
State Representative, Assemblyman, or Delegate	The Honorable William R. Blank House of Delegates Baltimore, Maryland	Dear Sir: *or* Dear Madam:	Dear Mr. Blank: *or* Dear Ms Blank:	Very truly yours,	Sincerely yours,
District Attorney	The Honorable William R. Blank District Attorney, Albany County County Courthouse Albany, New York	Dear Sir:	Dear Mr. Blank:	Very truly yours,	Sincerely yours,
Mayor of a city	The Honorable William R. Blank Mayor of Detroit Detroit, Michigan	Dear Sir: *or* Dear Madam:	Dear Mayor Blank:	Very truly yours,	Sincerely yours,

[2]In most states the lower branch of the legislature is the House of Representatives. The exceptions to this are: New York, California, Wisconsin and Nevada, where it is known as the Assembly; Maryland, Virginia, and West Virginia—the House of Delegates; New Jersey—the House of General Assembly.

STATE AND LOCAL GOVERNMENT OFFICIALS *continued*

Personage	Envelope and Inside Address	Formal Salutation	Informal Salutation	Formal Close	Informal Close
President of a Board of Commissioners	The Honorable William R. Blank, President Board of Commissioners of the City of Buffalo Buffalo, New York	Dear Sir:	Dear Mr. Blank:	Very truly yours,	Sincerely yours,
City Attorney City Counsel, Corporation Counsel	The Honorable William R. Blank, City Attorney (City Counsel, Corporation Counsel) San Francisco, California	Dear Sir:	Dear Mr. Blank:	Very truly yours,	Sincerely yours,
Alderman	Alderman William R. Blank City Hall Denver, Colorado	Dear Sir:	Dear Mr. Blank:	Very truly yours,	Sincerely yours,

COURT OFFICIALS

Personage	Envelope and Inside Address	Formal Salutation	Informal Salutation	Formal Close	Informal Close
Chief Justice[1] of a State Supreme Court	The Honorable William (or Nancy) R. Blank Chief Justice of the Supreme Court of Minnesota[2] Minneapolis, Minnesota	Sir: *or* Madam:	Dear Mr. Chief Justice: *or* Dear Ms Chief Justice:	Very truly yours,	Sincerely yours,
Associate Justice of a Supreme Court of a State	The Honorable William (or Nancy) R. Blank Associate Justice of the Supreme Court of Minnesota Minneapolis, Minnesota	Sir: *or* Madam:	Dear Justice Blank:	Very truly yours,	Sincerely yours,
Presiding Justice	The Honorable William (or Nancy) R. Blank Presiding Justice, Appellate Division Supreme Court of New York New York, New York	Sir: *or* Madam:	Dear Justice Blank:	Very truly yours,	Sincerely yours,
Judge of a Court[3]	The Honorable William (or Nancy) R. Blank Judge of the United States District Court for the Southern District of California Los Angeles, California	Sir: *or* Madam:	Dear Judge Blank:	Very truly yours,	Sincerely yours,
Clerk of a Court	William (or Nancy) R. Blank, Esquire Clerk of the Superior Court of Massachusetts Boston, Massachusetts	Dear Sir: *or* Dear Madam:	Dear Mr. Blank: *or* Dear Ms Blank:	Very truly yours,	Sincerely yours,

[1]If his official title is *Chief Judge* substitute *Chief Judge* for *Chief Justice*, but never use *Mr.* with *Chief Judge* or *Judge*.
[2]Substitute here the appropriate name of the court. For example, the highest court in New York State is called the Court of Appeals.
[3]Not applicable to judges of United States Supreme Court.

UNITED STATES DIPLOMATIC REPRESENTATIVES

Personage	Envelope and Inside Address	Formal Salutation	Informal Salutation	Formal Close	Informal Close
American Ambassador (man)	The Honorable William R. Blank American Ambassador[1] London, England	Sir:	Dear Mr. Ambassador:	Very truly yours,	Sincerely yours,
American Ambassador[3] (woman)	The Honorable Louise Blank American Ambassador London, England	Madam:	Dear Madam Ambassador:	Very truly yours,	Sincerely yours,
American Minister (man)	The Honorable William R. Blank American Minister Bucharest, Rumania	Sir:	Dear Mr. Minister:	Very truly yours,	Sincerely yours,
American Minister (woman)	The Honorable Louise Blank American Minister Bucharest, Rumania	Madam:	Dear Mrs. (Miss) Blank: *or* Dear Madam Minister:	Very truly yours,	Sincerely yours,
American Chargé d'Affaires ad interim (man)	William R. Blank, Esquire American Chargé d'Affaires ad interim (City, State)	Sir:	Dear Mr. Blank:	Very truly yours,	Sincerely yours,
American Chargé d'Affaires ad interim (woman)	Mrs. (Miss) Louise Blank American Chargé d'Affaires ad interim (City, State)	Madam:	Dear Mrs. (Miss) Blank:	Very truly yours,	Sincerely yours,
American Consul General, Consul, or Vice Consul	William R. Blank, Esquire American Consul General (Consul or Vice Consul) Warsaw	Sir:	Dear Mr. Blank:	Very truly yours,	Sincerely yours,
High Commissioner	The Honorable William R. Blank United States High Commissioner to Argentina Buenos Aires	Sir:	Dear Mr. Blank:	Very truly yours,	Sincerely yours,

[1]When an ambassador or minister is not at his post, the name of the country to which he is accredited must be added to the address. For example: "The American Ambassador to Great Britain." If he holds military rank, the diplomatic complimentary title "The Honorable" should be omitted, thus "General William R. Blank, American Ambassador (or Minister)."

[2]With reference to ambassadors and ministers to Central or South America countries, substitute *The Ambassador of the United States* for *American Ambassador* or *American Minister.*

[3]In addressing a woman ambassador or minister, the customary form of addressing a husband and his wife applies.

FOREIGN OFFICIALS AND REPRESENTATIVES

Personage	Envelope and Inside Address	Formal Salutation	Informal Salutation	Formal Close	Informal Close
Foreign Ambassador[1] in the United States	His Excellency,[2] Erik Rolf Blankson Ambassador of Norway Washington, D. C.	Excellency:	Dear Mr. Ambassador:	Respectfully yours,	Sincerely yours,
Foreign Minister[1] in the United States	The Honorable George Macovescu Minister of Rumania Washington, D. C.	Sir:	Dear Mr. Minister:	Respectfully yours,	Sincerely yours,
Foreign Diplomatic Representative with a Personal Title[3]	His Excellency,[4] Count Allesandro de Bianco Ambassador of Italy Washington, D. C.	Excellency:	Dear Mr. Ambassador:	Respectfully yours,	Sincerely yours,
Prime Minister	His Excellency, Christian Jawaharal Blank Prime Minister of India New Delhi, India	Excellency:	Dear Mr. Prime Minister:	Respectfully yours,	Sincerely yours,
British Prime Minister	The Right Honorable Godfrey Blank, K.G., M.C., M.P. Prime Minister London, England	Sir:	Dear Mr. Prime Minister: *or* Dear Mr. Blank:	Respectfully yours,	Sincerely yours,
Canadian Prime Minister	The Right Honorable Claude Louis St. Blanc, C.M.G. Prime Minister of Canada Ottawa, Canada	Sir:	Dear Mr. Prime Minister: *or* Dear Mr. Blanc:	Respectfully yours,	Sincerely yours,
President of a Republic	His Excellency, Juan Cuidad Blanco President of the Dominican Republic	Excellency:	Dear Mr. President:	I remain with respect, Very truly yours, (formal general usage) Sincerely yours, (less formal)	Sincerely yours,
Premier	His Excellency, Charles Yves de Blanc Premier of the French Republic Paris	Excellency:	Dear Mr. Premier:	Respectfully yours,	Sincerely yours,
Foreign Chargé d'Affaires (de missi)[5] in the United States	Mr. Jan Gustaf Blanc Chargé d'Affaires of Sweden Washington, D. C.	Sir:	Dear Mr. Blanc:	Respectfully yours,	Sincerely yours,
Foreign Chargé d'Affaires ad interim in the United States	Mr. Edmund Blank Chargé d'Affaires ad interim[6] of Ireland Washington, D. C.	Sir:	Dear Mr. Blank:	Respectfully yours,	Sincerely yours,

[1]The correct title of all ambassadors and ministers of foreign countries is "Ambassador (Minister) of _____" (name of country) with the exception of Great Britain. The adjective form is used with reference to representatives from Great Britain—*British Ambassador, British Minister. See* "British Forms—Government Officials," page 46

[2]When the representative is British or a member of the British Commonwealth, it is customary to use "The Right Honorable" and "The Honorable" in addition to "His Excellency," wherever appropriate.

[3]If the personal title is a royal title, such as "His Highness," "Prince," etc., the diplomatic title "His Excellency" or "The Honorable" is omitted.

[4]Dr., Señor Don, and other titles of special courtesy in Spanish-speaking countries may be used with the diplomatic title "His Excellency" or "The Honorable."

[5]The full title is usually shortened to chargé d'affaires.

[6]The words "ad interim" should not be omitted in the address.

THE ARMED FORCES / THE ARMY

Personage	Envelope and Inside Address	Formal Salutation	Informal Salutation	Formal Close	Informal Close
General of the Army[1]	General of the Army William R. Blank, U.S.A. Department of the Army Washington, D. C.	Sir:	Dear General Blank:	Very truly yours,	Sincerely yours,
General, Lieutenant General, Major General, Brigadier General	General (Lieutenant General, Major General or Brigadier General) William R. Blank, U.S.A.[2] Fort Leavenworth, Kansas	Sir:	Dear General Blank:	Very truly yours,	Sincerely yours,
Colonel, Lieutenant Colonel	Colonel (Lieutenant Colonel) William R. Blank, U.S.A. Fort Dix, New Jersey	Dear Colonel Blank:	Dear Colonel Blank:	Very truly yours,	Sincerely yours,
Major	Major William R. Blank, U.S.A. Fort Sam Houston, Texas	Dear Major Blank:	Dear Major Blank:	Very truly yours,	Sincerely yours,
Captain	Captain William R. Blank, U.S.A. Fort Shelby, Mississippi	Dear Captain Blank:	Dear Captain Blank:	Very truly yours,	Sincerely yours,
First Lieutenant, Second Lieutenant[3]	Lieutenant William R. Blank, U.S.A. Fort Schuyler, New York	Dear Lieutenant Blank:	Dear Lieutenant Blank:	Very truly yours,	Sincerely yours,
Chief Warrant Officer, Warrant Officer	Mr. William R. Blank, U.S.A. Fort Dix, New Jersey	Dear Mr. Blank:	Dear Mr. Blank:	Very truly yours,	Sincerely yours,
Chaplain in the U.S. Army[4]	Chaplain William R. Blank, Captain, U.S.A. Fort Sill, Oklahoma	Dear Chaplain Blank:	Dear Chaplain Blank:	Very truly yours,	Sincerely yours,

[1] At present there is no General of the Army in active service.
[2] *U.S.A.* indicates regular service. *A.U.S* (Army of the United States) signifies the Reserve.
[3] In all *official* correspondence the full rank should be included in both the envelope address and the inside address, but not in the salutation.
[4] Roman Catholic chaplains and certain Anglican priests are introduced as "*Chaplain Blank*" but are spoken to and referred to as "*Father Blank.*"

THE ARMED FORCES / THE NAVY

Personage	Envelope and Inside Address	Formal Salutation	Informal Salutation	Formal Close	Informal Close
Fleet Admiral	Fleet Admiral William R. Blank, U.S.N. Chief of Naval Operations Department of the Navy Washington, D. C.	Sir:	Dear Admiral Blank:	Very truly yours,	Sincerely yours,

Personage	Envelope and Inside Address	Formal Salutation	Informal Salutation	Formal Close	Informal Close
Admiral, Vice Admiral, Rear Admiral	Admiral (Vice Admiral or Rear Admiral) William R. Blank, U.S.N. United States Naval Academy[1] Annapolis, Maryland	Sir:	Dear Admiral Blank:	Very truly yours,	Sincerely yours,
Commodore, Captain, Commander, Lieutenant Commander	Commodore (Captain, Commander, Lieutenant Commander) William R. Blank, U.S.N. U.S.S. Mississippi San Diego, California	Dear Commodore (Captain, Commander) Blank:	Dear Commodore (Captain, Commander) Blank:	Very truly yours,	Sincerely yours,
Junior Officers: Lieutenant, Lieutenant Junior Grade, Ensign	(Lieutenant, etc.) William R. Blank, U.S.N. U.S.S. Wyoming Norfolk, Virginia	Dear Mr. Blank:	Dear Mr. Blank:	Very truly yours,	Sincerely yours,
Chief Warrant Officer, Warrant Officer	Mr. William R. Blank, U.S.N. U.S.S. Texas San Diego, California	Dear Mr. Blank:	Dear Mr. Blank:	Very truly yours,	Sincerely yours,
Chaplain	Chaplain William R. Blank Captain, U.S.N. Department of the Navy Washington, D. C.	Dear Chaplain Blank:	Dear Chaplain Blank:	Very truly yours,	Sincerely yours,

[1] U.S.N. signifies regular service; U.S.N.R. indicates the Reserve.

THE ARMED FORCES — AIR FORCE

Air Force titles are the same as those in the Army, *U.S.A.F.* is used instead of *U.S.A.*, and *A.F.U.S.* is used to indicate the Reserve.

THE ARMED FORCES — MARINE CORPS

Marine Corps titles are the same as those in the Army, except that the top rank is *Commandant of the Marine Corps. U.S.M.C.* indicates regular service, *U.S.M.R.* indicates the Reserve.

THE ARMED FORCES — COAST GUARD

Coast Guard titles are the same as those in the Navy, except that the top rank is Admiral. *U.S.C.G.* indicates regular service, *U.S.C.G.R.* indicates the Reserve.

CHURCH DIGNITARIES / CATHOLIC FAITH

Personage	Envelope and Inside Address	Formal Salutation	Informal Salutation	Formal Close	Informal Close
The Pope	His Holiness The Pope *or* His Holiness Pope John XXIII Vatican City	Your Holiness:	*Always Formal*	Respectfully,	*Always Formal*
Apostolic Delegate	His Excellency, The Most Reverend William R. Blank: Archbishop of _____, The Apostolic Delegate Washington, D. C.	Your Excellency:	My dear Archbishop:	Respectfully yours,	Respectfully,
Cardinal in the United States	His Eminence, William Cardinal Blank Archbishop of New York New York, New York	Your Eminence:	*Always Formal*	Respectfully yours,	Respectfully, *or* Sincerely yours,
Archbishop in the United States	The Most Reverend William R. Blank, D.D. Archbishop of Baltimore Baltimore, Maryland	Your Excellency:	Dear Archbishop Blank:	Respectfully yours,	Respectfully, *or* Sincerely yours,
Bishop in the United States	The Most Reverend William R. Blank, D.D. Bishop of Boston Boston, Massachusetts	Your Excellency:	Dear Bishop Blank:	Respectfully yours,	Sincerely yours,
Bishop in England	The Right Reverend William R. Blank Bishop of Sussex (local address)	Right Reverend Sir:	Dear Bishop:	Respectfully yours,	Respectfully,
Abbot	The Right Reverend William R. Blank Abbot of Westmoreland Abbey Washington, D. C.	Dear Father Abbot:	Dear Father Blank:	Respectfully yours,	Sincerely yours,
Canon	The Reverend William R. Blank, D.D. Canon of St. Patrick's Cathedral New York, New York	Dear Canon Blank:	Dear Canon Blank:	Respectfully yours,	Sincerely yours,
Monsignor	The Right (or Very)[1] Reverend Msgr. William R. Blank Boston, Massachusetts	Right Reverend and Dear Monsignor Blank: *or* Very Reverend and Dear Monsignor Blank:	Dear Monsignor Blank:	Respectfully yours,	Sincerely yours,

[1]Dependent upon rank. See the *Official* (Roman) *Catholic Directory.*

CHURCH DIGNITARIES / CATHOLIC FAITH *continued*

Personage	Envelope and Inside Address	Formal Salutation	Informal Salutation	Formal Close	Informal Close
Brother	Brother John Francis 932 Maple Avenue San Francisco, California	Dear Brother Francis:	Dear Brother Francis:	Respectfully yours,	Sincerely yours,
Superior of a Brotherhood and Priest[2]	The Very Reverend William R. Blank, M.M. Director Birchknoll, New York	Dear Father Superior:	Dear Father Superior:	Respectfully yours,	Sincerely yours,
Priest	*With Scholastic Degree* The Reverend William R. Blank, Ph.D. Georgetown University Washington, D. C.	Dear Dr. Blank:	Dear Dr. Blank:	Respectfully,	Sincerely yours,
	Without Scholastic Degree The Reverend William R. Blank St. Vincent's Church Lynchburg, Virginia	Dear Father Blank:	Dear Father Blank:	Respectfully,	Sincerely yours,
Sister Superior	The Reverend Sister Superior (order, if used)[3] Convent of the Sacred Heart Sacramento, California	Dear Sister Superior:	Dear Sister Superior:	Respectfully,	Respectfully,
Sister	Sister Mary Magdelena St. John's High School Northfield, Maine	Dear Sister:	Dear Sister Mary Magdelena:	Respectfully,	Sincerely yours,

[2]The address for the superior of a Brotherhood depends upon whether or not he is a priest or has a title other than superior. Consult the *Official Catholic Directory.*
[3]The address of the superior of a Sisterhood depends upon the order to which she belongs. The abbreviation of the order is not always used. Consult the *Official Catholic Directory.*

CHURCH DIGNITARIES / JEWISH FAITH

Personage	Envelope and Inside Address	Formal Salutation	Informal Salutation	Formal Close	Informal Close
Rabbi	*With scholastic degree* Rabbi William R. Blank, Ph.D. *or* Dr. William R. Blank	Sir:	Dear Rabbi Blank: *or* Dear Dr. Blank:	Respectfully,	Sincerely yours,
	Without scholastic degree Rabbi William R. Blank	Sir:	Dear Rabbi Blank:	Respectfully,	Sincerely yours,

CHURCH DIGNITARIES / PROTESTANT FAITH

Personage	Envelope and Inside Address	Formal Salutation	Informal Salutation	Formal Close	Informal Close
Archbishop (Anglican)	To His Grace The Lord Archbishop of Canterbury Canterbury, England	Your Grace: *or* My Lord Arch- bishop:	My dear Archbishop:	Respectfully yours,	Sincerely yours,
Presiding Bishop of the Protestant Episcopal Church in America	The Most Reverend William R. Blank, D.D., LL.D. Presiding Bishop of the Protestant Episcopal Church in America Northwick House Northwick, Connecticut	Most Reverend Sir:	Dear Bishop: *or* Dear Bishop Blank:	Respectfully yours,	Sincerely yours,
Anglican Bishop	The Right Reverend The Lord Bishop of London London, England	My Lord Bishop:	My dear Bishop:	Respectfully yours,	Sincerely yours,
Methodist Bishop	The Reverend William R. Blank Methodist Bishop Phoenix, Arizona	Reverend Sir:	Dear Bishop Blank:	Respectfully yours,	Sincerely yours,
Protestant Episcopal Bishop	The Right Reverend the Bishop of Denver *or* The Right Reverend William R. Blank, D.D., LL.D. Bishop of Denver Denver, Colorado	Right Reverend Sir:	Dear Bishop Blank:	Respectfully yours,	Sincerely yours,
Anglican Archdeacon	The Venerable William R. Blank The Archdeacon of Baltimore Baltimore, Maryland	Venerable Sir:	My dear Archdeacon:	Respectfully yours,	Sincerely yours,
Protestant Episcopal Archdeacon	The Venerable William R. Blank, D.D. The Archdeacon of Wilmington Wilmington, Delaware	Venerable Sir:	My Dear Archdeacon:	Respectfully yours,	Sincerely yours,
Dean[1]	The Very Reverend William R. Blank, D.D. Dean of St. John's Cathedral Chicago, Illinois	Dear Dean Blank:	Dear Dean Blank:	Respectfully,	Sincerely yours,

[1]Applies only to the head of a Cathedral or of a Theological Seminary.

CHURCH DIGNITARIES / PROTESTANT FAITH *continued*

Personage	Envelope and Inside Address	Formal Salutation	Informal Salutation	Formal Close	Informal Close
Protestant Minister	*With scholastic degree* The Reverend William R. Blank, D.D., Litt.D. Delta, Mississippi	Dear Dr. Blank:	Dear Dr. Blank:	Very truly yours,	Sincerely yours,
	Without scholastic degree The Reverend William R. Blank Rochester, New York	Dear Mr. Blank:	Dear Mr. Blank:	Very truly yours,	Sincerely yours,
Episcopal Priest (High Church)	*With scholastic degree* The Reverend William R. Blank, D.D., Litt.D. All Saint's Cathedral Hartford, Connecticut	Dear Dr. Blank:	Dear Dr. Blank:	Very truly yours,	Sincerely yours,
	Without scholastic degree The Reverend William R. Blank St. Paul's Church Houston, Texas	Dear Mr. Blank: *or* Dear Father Blank:	Dear Mr. Blank: *or* Dear Father Blank:	Very truly yours,	Sincerely yours,

COLLEGE AND UNIVERSITY OFFICIALS

Personage	Envelope and Inside Address	Formal Salutation	Informal Salutation	Formal Close	Informal Close
President of a College or University	*With a doctor's degree* William R. Blank, LL.D., Ph.D. *or* Mary R. Blank, Ph.D. *or* Dr. William R. Blank President, Amherst College Amherst, Massachusetts	Sir: *or* Madam:	Dear Dr. Blank:	Very truly yours,	Sincerely yours,
	Without a doctor's degree Mr. William R. Blank President, Columbia University New York, New York *or* Mary R. Blank, President, Columbia University New York, New York	Sir: *or* Madam:	Dear President Blank:	Very truly yours,	Sincerely yours,
	Catholic Priest The Very Reverend William R. Blank, S.J., D.D., Ph.D. President, Fordham University New York, New York	Sir:	Dear Father Blank:	Very truly yours,	Sincerely yours,
University Chancellor	Dr. William R. Blank Chancellor, University of Alabama University, Alabama	Sir:	Dear Dr. Blank:	Very truly yours,	Sincerely yours,

COLLEGE AND UNIVERSITY OFFICIALS *continued*

Personage	Envelope and Inside Address	Formal Salutation	Informal Salutation	Formal Close	Informal Close
Dean or Assistant Dean of a College or Graduate School	Dean William R. Blank School of Law *or* (If he holds a doctor's degree) Dr. William R. Blank, Dean (Assistant Dean), School of Law University of Virginia Charlottesville, Virginia	Dear Sir: *or* Dear Dean Blank:	Dear Dean Blank:	Very truly yours,	Sincerely yours,
Dean of a College for Women	Dean Mary Louise Blank Smith College *or* (If she holds a doctor's degree) Dr. Mary Louise Blank Dean, Smith College Northhampton, Massachusetts	Dear Madam: *or* Dear Dean Blank:	Dear Dean Blank:	Very truly yours,	Sincerely yours,
Professor	Professor William R. Blank *or* (If he holds a doctor's degree) William R. Blank, Ph.D. Yale University New Haven, Connecticut	Dear Sir: *or* Dear Madam: *or* Dear Professor (Dr.) Blank:	Dear Professor (Dr.) Blank:	Very truly yours,	Sincerely yours,
Associate or Assistant Professor	Mr. William R. Blank *or* (If he holds a doctor's degree) William R. Blank, Ph.D. Associate (Assistant) Professor Department of Romance Languages Williams College Williamstown, Massachusetts	Dear Sir: *or* Dear Madam: *or* Dear Professor (Dr.) Blank:	Dear Professor (Dr.) Blank:	Very truly yours,	Sincerely yours,
Instructor	Mr. William R. Blank *or* (If he holds a doctor's degree) William R. Blank, Ph.D. Department of Economics University of California Berkeley, California	Dear Sir: *or* Dear Madam: *or* Dear Mr. (Dr.) Blank:	Dear Mr. (Dr.) Blank: *or* Dear Ms (Dr.) Blank:	Very truly yours,	Sincerely yours,
Chaplain of a College or University	The Reverend William R. Blank, D.D. Chaplain, Trinity College Hartford, Connecticut *or* Chaplain William R. Blank Trinity College Hartford, Connecticut	Dear Chaplain Blank: *or* (If he holds a doctor's degree) Dear Dr. Blank:	Dear Chaplain (Dr.) Blank:	Very truly yours,	Sincerely yours,

THE UNITED NATIONS[1]

Personage	Envelope and Inside Address	Formal Salutation	Informal Salutation	Formal Close	Informal Close
Secretary General	His Excellency, William R. Blank Secretary General of the United Nations New York 16, New York	Excellency:[2]	Dear Mr. Secretary General:	Very truly yours,	Sincerely yours,
Under Secretary	The Honorable William R. Blank Under Secretary of the United Nations The Secretariat United Nations New York 16, New York	Sir:	Dear Mr. Blank:	Very truly yours,	Sincerely yours,
Foreign Representative (with Ambassadorial rank)	His *or* Her Excellency, William R. Blank Representative of Spain to the United Nations New York 16, New York	Excellency: *or* Madam:	Dear Mr. Ambassador: *or* Dear Madam Ambassador:	Very truly yours,	Sincerely yours,
United States Representative (with Ambassadorial rank)	The Honorable William R. Blank United States Representative to the United Nations New York 16, New York	Sir: *or* Dear Mr. Ambassador: *or* Madam:	Dear Mr. Ambassador: *or* Dear Madam Ambassador:	Very truly yours,	Sincerely yours,
United States Representative to the Economic and Social Council	The Honorable William R. Blank United States Representative to the Economic and Social Council of the United Nations New York 16, New York	Sir:	Dear Mr. Blank:	Very truly yours,	Sincerely yours,
United States Representative to the Trusteeship Council	The Honorable William R. Blank United States Representative to the Trusteeship Council of the United Nations New York 16, New York	Sir:	Dear Mr. Blank:	Very truly yours,	Sincerely yours,
Senior Representative of the United States to the General Assembly	The Honorable William R. Blank Senior Representative of the United States to the General Assembly of the United Nations New York 16, New York	Sir:	Dear Mr. Blank:	Very truly yours,	Sincerely yours,

[1]The six principal branches through which the United Nations functions are The General Assembly, The Security Council, The Economic and Social Council, The Trusteeship Council, The International Court of Justice, and The Secretariat.
[2]An American citizen should never be addressed as "Excellency."

THE ORGANIZATION OF AMERICAN STATES[1]

Personage	Envelope and Inside Address	Formal Salutation	Informal Salutation	Formal Close	Informal Close
Secretary General	The Honorable William R. Blank Secretary General of the Organization of American States Pan American Union Washington 6, D. C.	Sir:	Dear Mr. Secretary General:	Very truly yours,	Sincerely yours,
Assistant Secretary General	The Honorable William R. Blank Assistant Secretary General of the Organization of American States Pan American Union Washington 6, D. C.	Sir:	Dear Mr. Blank:	Very truly yours,	Sincerely yours,
Foreign Representative (with Ambassadorial rank)	His *or* Her Excellency, William R. Blank Representative of Brazil on the Council of the Organization of American States (local address)	Excellency: *or* Madam:	Dear Mr. Ambassador: *or* Dear Madam Ambassador:	Very truly yours,	Sincerely yours,
United States Representative (with Ambassadorial rank)	The Honorable William R. Blank United States Representative on the Council of the Organization of American States Department of State Washington 25, D. C.	Sir: *or* Madam:	Dear Mr. Blank: *or* Dear Ms Blank:	Very truly yours,	Sincerely yours,

[1]The six branches through which the Organization of American States function are The Inter-American Conference, The Meeting of Consultation of Ministers of Foreign Affairs, The Council, The Pan-American Union, The Specialized Conferences, and The Specialized Organizations.

MISCELLANEOUS

Personage	Envelope and Inside Address	Formal Salutation	Informal Salutation	Formal Close	Informal Close
Doctor	Dr. William R. Blank[1] (local address)	Dear Dr. Blank:	Dear Dr. Blank:	Very truly yours,	Sincerely yours,
Lawyer	Mr. William R. Blank[2] Attorney at Law (local address)	Dear Mr. Blank: *or* Dear Ms Blank:	Dear Mr. Blank: *or* Dear Ms Blank:	Very truly yours,	Sincerely yours,

[1]It is permissible to address a doctor as *William R. Blank, M.D.* (or *D.D.S.*, or *Ph.D.*, as the case may be) but the form in the chart is preferable.
[2]*Esquire* or *Esq.* may be used to address prominent attorneys or other high ranking professional men who do not have titles. When *Esquire* or *Esq.* is used, *Mr.* does not precede the name. A lawyer generally addresses another lawyer as *Esquire*, and many lawyers also use the title in addressing their clients. There is no feminine of *esquire;* the word is never used in addressing women.

MISCELLANEOUS *continued*

Personage	Envelope and Inside Address	Formal Salutation	Informal Salutation	Formal Close	Informal Close
Law Firm[3]	Blank, Blank, and Blank Attorneys at Law (local address)	Gentlemen:	Gentlemen:	Very truly yours,	Sincerely yours,
School Principal	*(With a doctor's degree)* Dr. William R. Blank *or* William R. Blank, Ph.D. Principal, Lincoln High School Lincoln, Kansas	Dear Dr. Blank:	Dear Dr. Blank:	Very truly yours,	Sincerely yours,
	(Without a doctor's degree) Mr. William R. Blank Principal, Lincoln High School Lincoln, Kansas	Dear Mr. Blank: *or* Dear Ms Blank:	Dear Mr. Blank: *or* Dear Ms Blank:	Very truly yours,	Sincerely yours,
Company or a Corporation	William Blank and Company, Inc. (local address)	Gentlemen:	Gentlemen:	Very truly yours,	Sincerely yours,
Corporation (attention of an individual)	William Blank and Company, Inc. (local address) Attention: Mr. John Blank	Gentlemen:	Gentlemen:	Very truly yours,	Sincerely yours,
Federation	Mr. William R. Blank, President American Federation of Industry (local address)	Dear Sir:	Dear Mr. Blank:	Very truly yours,	Sincerely yours,
Group of Men and Women	The Gulf Sailing Club (local address)	Ladies and Gentlemen:	Ladies and Gentlemen:	Very truly yours,	Sincerely yours,
Two or More Individuals	*Men* Mr. William R. Blank and Mr. Kenneth Doe 974 Atlanta Avenue Boston, Massachusetts	Gentlemen:	Dear Mr. Blank and Mr. Doe:	Very truly yours,	Sincerely yours,
	Women Mrs. William R. Blank, Ms Kenneth Doe, and Miss Louise Doe (local address)	Mesdames:	Dear Mrs. Blank and Ms Doe:	Very truly yours,	Sincerely yours,
Married Woman in Business[4]	Mrs. Louise Blank *or* Ms Louise Blank	Dear Mrs. Blank:	Dear Mrs. Blank: *or* Dear Ms Blank:	Very truly yours,	Sincerely yours,
Widow	Mrs. Janice R. Blank (local address)	Dear Mrs. Blank:	Dear Mrs. Blank:	Very truly yours,	Sincerely yours,
Divorcee	Mrs. Janice Blank[5] (local address) *or* Ms Janice Blank (local address)	Dear Mrs. Blank: *or* Dear Ms Blank:	Dear Mrs. Blank: *or* Dear Ms Blank:	Very truly yours,	Sincerely yours,

[3]A firm of attorneys may be addressed as *Messers* or as *Esquires,* but the form in the chart is preferable because frequently the firm name is not similar to the names of the partners—often the firm name continues to include the name of a deceased partner.

[4]A married woman in business may use her husband's name for business purposes, but the form in the chart is more usual.

[5]A divorcee uses her full surname followed by that of her former husband. If her surname is similar to a given name, thus resulting in an unfortunate combination of names, she may use the initial of her given name, her surname, and the surname of her former husband (see second example in chart).

BRITISH FORMS / THE PEERAGE,[1] BARONETS AND KNIGHTS

Personage	Envelope and Inside Address	Formal Salutation	Informal Salutation	Formal Close	Informal Close
Duke[2]	The Duke of Milbank (local address)	Sir:	Dear Duke:[3]	Very truly yours,	Sincerely yours,
Duchess	The Duchess of Milbank (local address)	Madam:	Dear Duchess:	Very truly yours,	Sincerely yours,
The Younger Son of a Duke	The Lord Geoffrey Thurston (local address)	Sir:	Dear Lord Geoffrey:	Very truly yours,	Sincerely yours,
Wife of a Younger Son of a Duke	The Lady Geoffrey Thurston (local address)	Madam:	Dear Lady Geoffrey:	Very truly yours,	Sincerely yours,
Daughter of a Duke	The Lady Patricia Thurston (local address)	Madam:	Dear Lady Patricia:	Very truly yours,	Sincerely yours,
Widow of a Duke[4]	Jessica, Duchess of Milbank (local address)	Madam:	Dear Duchess:	Very truly yours,	Sincerely yours,
Marquess[5]	The Marquess of Brainbridge (local address)	Sir:	Dear Lord Brainbridge:	Very truly yours,	Sincerely yours,
Marchioness	The Marchioness of Brainbridge (local address)	Madam:	Dear Lady Brainbridge:	Very truly yours,	Sincerely yours,
Earl[6][7]	The Earl of Ashton (local address)	Sir:	Dear Lord Ashton:	Very truly yours,	Sincerely yours,
Countess (Wife of an Earl)	The Countess of Ashton (local address)	Madam:	Dear Lady Ashton:	Very truly yours,	Sincerely yours,
A Younger Son of an Earl	The Hon. Laurence Horne[8] (local address)	Sir:	Dear Mr. Horne:	Very truly yours,	Sincerely yours,
Wife of a Younger Son of an Earl	The Hon. Mrs. Laurence Horne (local address)	Madam:	Dear Mrs. Horne:	Very truly yours,	Sincerely yours,
Viscount[9]	The Viscount Trabert (local address)	Sir:	Dear Lord Trabert:	Very truly yours,	Sincerely yours,

[1]The eldest son of a Peer takes the highest family title below that of his father.

[2]See note (1). The eldest son of a Duke takes the title *Marquess.* His wife takes the corresponding title *Marchioness.*

[3]While the salutation *My dear* is often selected in the United States for formal correspondence, it is used in England only between intimate friends.

[4]A woman divorced from a Peer is addressed as though she were his widow until she remarries.

[5]The eldest son of a Marquess takes the title *Earl.* His wife takes the corresponding title *Countess.* The forms of address of the younger sons and the daughters of a Marquess are the same as for *Younger Son of a Duke* and *Daughter of a Duke.* See these forms. The wife of a younger son of a Marquess takes the title *Lady* with her husband's full name.

[6]The eldest son of an Earl takes the title *Viscount.* His wife takes the corresponding title *Viscountess.*

[7]The forms of address for the daughter of an Earl are the same as for *Daughter of a Duke.*

[8]"Honorable" is always abbreviated in British usage.

[9]The sons of a Viscount and their wives take the title "Honorable." See the forms for *Younger Son of an Earl* and *Wife of a Younger Son of an Earl.*

BRITISH FORMS / THE PEERAGE, BARONETS AND KNIGHTS *continued*

Personage	Envelope and Inside Address	Formal Salutation	Informal Salutation	Formal Close	Informal Close
Viscountess	The Viscountess Trabert (local address)	Madam:	Dear Lady Trabert:	Very truly yours,	Sincerely yours,
Daughter of a Viscount	The Hon. Gwendolyn Trabert (local address)	Madam:	Dear Miss Trabert:	Very truly yours,	Sincerely yours,
Widow of a Marquess, an Earl, or a Viscount	Jessica, Marchioness (Countess, Viscountess) of Brainbridge (local address)	Madam:	Dear Lady Brainbridge:	Very truly yours,	Sincerely yours,
Baron[10]	The Lord Carlton (local address)	Sir:	Dear Lord Carlton:	Very truly yours,	Sincerely yours,
Baroness	The Lady Carlton (local address)	Madam:	Dear Lady Carlton:	Very truly yours,	Sincerely yours,
Widow of a Baron	Penelope, Baroness Carlton (local address)	Madam:	Dear Lady Carlton:	Very truly yours,	Sincerely yours,
Baronet[11]	Sir Bramwell Wilding, Bart. (local address)	Sir:	Dear Sir Bramwell:	Very truly yours,	Sincerely yours,
Wife of a Baronet	Lady Wilding (local address)	Madam:	Dear Lady Wilding:	Very truly yours,	Sincerely yours,
Knight	Sir Randall Powell (local address)	Sir:	Dear Sir Randall:	Very truly yours,	Sincerely yours,
Widow of a Baronet or Knight	Margaret, Lady Wilding (local address)	Madam:	Dear Lady Wilding:	Very truly yours,	Sincerely yours,

[10]The sons of a Baron and their wives also take the title "Honorable," as do the daughters of a Baron.
[11]The sons and daughters of a Baronet are not titled.

BRITISH FORMS / GOVERNMENT OFFICIALS

Personage	Envelope and Inside Address	Formal Salutation	Informal Salutation	Formal Close	Informal Close
Prime Minister (with title)	The Rt. Hon. Sir William Bartlett, K.G., O.M., C.H., M.P. Prime Minister No. 10 Downing Street London, England	Dear Mr. Prime Minister: *or* Dear Madam Prime Minister:	Dear Sir William: *or* Dear Madam William:	Respectfully,	Very truly yours, *or* Sincerely yours,

BRITISH FORMS / GOVERNMENT OFFICIALS *continued*

Personage	Envelope and Inside Address	Formal Salutation	Informal Salutation	Formal Close	Informal Close
Prime Minister (without title)	The Rt. Hon. William Bartlett, P.C., M.P. Prime Minister No. 10 Downing Street London, England	Dear Mr. Prime Minister: *or* Dear Ms Prime Minister:	Dear Mr. Bartlett: *or* Dear Ms Bartlett:	Respectfully,	Very truly yours, *or* Sincerely yours,
Secretary of State for Foreign Affairs	The Rt. Hon. Sumner Tilden Secretary of State for Foreign Affairs London, England	Dear Sir:	Dear Mr. Tilden:	Very truly yours,	Sincerely yours,
Lord Chief Justice	The Rt. Hon. The Lord Chief Justice of England London, England	Dear Sir:	Dear Lord Chief Justice:	Very truly yours,	Sincerely yours,
Lord Chancellor	The Rt. Hon. The Lord High Chancellor *or* The Rt. Hon. Selwyn Reade Lord High Chancellor (local address)	Dear Sir:	Dear Lord Chancellor:	Very truly yours,	Sincerely yours,
Member of the House of Lords	The Rt. Hon. The Earl of Ashton[1] House of Lords London, England	Dear Sir:	Dear Lord Ashton:	Very truly yours,	Sincerely yours,
Member of the House of Commons	*With title* The Rt. Hon. Sir Winston Nordell, K.B.E., M.P. House of Commons London, England	Dear Sir:	Dear Sir Winston:	Very truly yours,	Sincerely yours,
	Without title Winston Nordell, Esq., M.P. House of Commons London, England	Dear Sir:	Dear Mr. Nordell:	Very truly yours,	Sincerely yours,
Privy Councillor	*With title* The Rt. Hon. Sir Clyde Wescott, Bart. (local address)	Dear Sir:	Dear Sir Clyde:	Very truly yours,	Sincerely yours,
	Without title The Rt. Hon. Clyde Wescott[2] (local address)	Dear Sir:	Dear Mr. Wescott:	Very truly yours,	Sincerely yours,
Lord Mayor	The Rt. Hon. The Lord Mayor of London *or* The Rt. Hon. Barton Tyne Lord Mayor of London London, England	Dear Sir:	Dear Lord Mayor:	Very truly yours,	Sincerely yours,

[1]Members of Parliament should be addressed according to rank of nobility. The address should contain the initials of their decorations or orders, if any, as well as *M.P.*, which may be omitted.

[2]The initials P.C. are generally omitted. In the case of a commoner, the complimentary title "The Right Honorable" sufficiently indicates he is a member of the Privy Council.

BRITISH FORMS / GOVERNMENT OFFICIALS *continued*

Personage	Envelope and Inside Address	Formal Salutation	Informal Salutation	Formal Close	Informal Close
British Ambassador	His Excellency, The Rt. Hon. Lord Cecil, P.C., G.C.M.G. British Ambassador Washington, D. C. *or* His Excellency, H.B.M. Ambassador British Embassy Washington, D. C.	Your Excellency:	Dear Mr. Ambassador: *or* Dear Madam Ambassador:	Very truly yours,	Sincerely yours,
Governor-General of a Dominion or Colony	*Without military rank* His Excellency, The Lord Sutherland Governor-Genéral of Ceylon Colombo	Dear Governor-General	Dear Lord Sutherland:	Very truly yours,	Sincerely yours,
	With military rank His Excellency, Colonel the Rt. Hon. G. Townsend Cunningham Governor-General of Ceylon Colombo	Dear Governor-General	Dear Colonel Cunningham:	Very truly yours,	Sincerely yours,